Conker Editions Ltd
22 Cosby Road
Littlethorpe
Leicester
LE19 2HF
Email: books@conkereditions.co.uk
Website: www.conkereditions.co.uk
First published by Conker Editions Ltd 2020.
A CIP catalogue record for this book is available from the British Library.
13-digit ISBN: 9781999900847.
Design and typesetting by Richard Johnson and Gary Silke.
Printed in the UK by Mixam.

The A-Z of Weird & Wonderful Football Shirts

Broccoli, Beer & Bruised Bananas

Richard Johnson

Foreword

by John Devlin

Richard Johnson clearly has an eye for the unusual, as well as a great love of collecting football shirts. This book presents the very best of his collection and is proof positive that the original requirement of the humble football jersey (simply to tell the two teams apart on a pitch) has now been superseded by a much wider remit. Obviously, shirts still need to clearly indicate to players, officials and spectators who's who, but actually the modern football shirt is a powerful, symbolic cultural item that fulfils many purposes and allows designers to flex their creative muscles.

Interest in football apparel has skyrocketed in recent years; an interest fuelled by the past. Football is inherently a nostalgic sport and the playing kit is now regarded as the signifying icon of these past 'rose-tinted' times, with interest in past kits ironically now standing shoulder to shoulder with interest in past players! It was this ethos I followed with my *True Colours* books. Current strips plunder history for inspiration, and the cycle of design is once again relying on pattern, heavy decoration and bold creativity.

Richard's carefully curated collection as presented in these pages illustrates the more adventurous side of football kit design. Granted, as these pages show, he has a penchant

for the garish, the novelty and in some cases the downright ugly, but his genuine passion for all aspects of the modern-day football shirt phenomenon is clear to see, with all jerseys presented with equal reverence and focus.

The book is packed with curios and the mystery and magic of foreign shirts – emblazoned with exotic sponsors' logos; shirts with outrageous sublimated patterns that are used as a marketing tool or for fund-raising purposes; rare, original shirts that I guarantee you will never have seen before; and immaculately recreated limited-edition anniversary shirts that directly reference momentous occasions in a club's history.

But it's not all novelty and shock – alongside the more unusual examples Richard studies and presents from his extensive collection are some rock-solid, *bona fide* kit classics that are quite simply great, iconic designs.

The A-Z of Weird & Wonderful

Football Shirts celebrates the unique, fascinating and unusual side of contemporary kit design – you'll never look at a football shirt the same way again...

John Devlin
www.truecoloursfootballkits.com
February 2020

Introduction

by Richard Johnson

I got my first football shirt at the age of 12, but my interest in kits had started long before that. As soon as the 1986 World Cup in Mexico had caused me to fall in love with football, I'd cherished the different outfits the players wore. The brilliant Mexico sun brought out the best of matches like Brazil-France – bright yellow against pure blue – and Argentina in sky blue and white stripes contrasting with the vibrant green of West Germany in the final. And then there was Denmark's iconic red half-and-half design.

On the domestic front, new fabric and manufacturing techniques meant the classic cotton look of the 60s and 70s was finally being replaced by a raft of shadow patterns and silky fabrics, perfectly mirroring the glitzy era that was the 80s.

In the following decade, the kit world continued its philosophy of 'if it can be done, then it shall be done'. Out went any last vestiges of minimalism and loud and garish sublimation was the order of the day, along with ultra-baggy shirts.

Save for the end-of-season ritual of buying the latest Coventry City shirt for a tenner, and finally getting my hands on an Argentina shirt, my collection didn't grow much at all during the 90s.

In the 2000s, two things happened that caused the collection to expand rapidly. Firstly, I discovered eBay. For a long time I proudly proclaimed that my first ever eBay purchase, nearly 20 years ago, was the Argentina shirt you see here. More recently, I downloaded my PayPal history and it turns out it was the second purchase – the first was actually the Add N to (X) CD single, 'Plug Me In'. The second inspirational factor was Italy's gorgeous 2006 World Cup shirt. Having not bought a brand-new shirt since

Coventry's 98-99 home shirt, I just had to have this one. Once that barrier was lifted, the shirt floodgates well and truly opened. At a time when online stores such as Subside, Kitbag and Classic Football Shirts were springing up, I was doomed.

But what caused my obsession with the more extreme end of the football shirt spectrum? Right from the beginning I'd admired the creativity of shirts like those of Denmark 86, Netherlands 88 and others of the early 90s. When La Hoya Lorca created their broccoli shirt, it crossed a line and I was fully on board. With each new all-over print, the increasing ire of the majority of fans just made me love them all the more. In a world of endless 'Big Three' templates, there's certainly a place for a sausage or a Cuban revolutionary.

So where does this leave the future of football shirts? The last few years have seen a rise in the number of top-tier teams releasing mash-up shirts and change shirts with prints on. This is hardly surprising, given that kits now only last a year and teams often release third, fourth and even fifth shirts as well as specials for cups or European tournaments. And let's not forget anniversary shirts! This growth in output forces designers to find new ways of keeping things fresh, but also gives them more

canvases on which to experiment.

Further muddying the waters is the increased prevalence of the pre-match shirt as a source of revenue, with England's 2018, Admiral-esque jersey garnering much attention from both fans and media. Manchester United's 'Chinese New Year' pre-match shirt was also much talked about, despite being in effect nothing more than a leisure shirt. Will these items soon be regarded as part of the official kit? Or will we see an increase in the number of shirts marketed as kit but never actually used, like the blackout shirts of the last few seasons?

How sustainable this kit explosion is remains to be seen, but while there's collectors like me around, there'll always be a market for the weird and wonderful.

SHAW CARPETS

MLS All-Stars
2017 Home

Every year since the MLS's inaugural season in 1996, it has held an All-Star match. Initially this was between the East and West Coast teams but, since 2005, it has pitted a combined MLS team against a club from Europe.

For the 2017 match, the All-Stars faced Real Madrid. With the scores level at 1-1 after 90 minutes, it went straight to penalties, which the visitors won 4-2.

The All-Star jersey changes every year and, for 2017, they opted for a tribute to the away shirt the US wore at World Cup 94 (the match was played at Soldier Field, which hosted the opening match of USA 94) - though with the addition of several maple leaves to represent the Canadian teams who play in the MLS.

Airdrieonians
2016-17 Mark Allison Tribute

In November 2014, lifelong Airdrieonians fan Mark Allison was diagnosed with pancreatic cancer and given six months to live. In response to this devastating news, Mark set up a F**k Cancer campaign and dedicated his time to raising money for cancer charities. By the time he sadly passed, over two years later in June 2017 and aged only 49, he had raised almost £80,000.

In honour of superfan Mark, the Supporters' Trust became the sponsor and featured an image of him on the shirt. The initial batch of 100 shirts sold out after 35 minutes, of which several were auctioned off for charity after being signed by celebrities such as Mark Hamill and Ricky Gervais. A second batch of 200 was made, selling to fans all over the UK.

Almost Famous

Le Coq Sportif
1986 Template

As you'll see elsewhere in this book, I have a fascination with famous shirts that also appeared around the world, often in lower leagues, as they were standard teamwear templates at the time. The Adidas Ipswich (Netherlands 88) and Hummel Mexico (Denmark 86) are prime examples.

The above shirt is a standard Le Coq Sportif template shirt from around 1986, but this particular example owes its place here to the Argentina shirt shown alongside, the full story of which can be found in World Cup Classics.

This incarnation shows what could have been had Brazil opted out of their distinctive Topper kit and followed their rivals' lead in the Mexican sun.

Kawasaki Frontale
2016 20th Anniversary 'Space Brothers' Special

Japanese kits tend towards the crazier end of the spectrum, so what does a club do when it wants to make a splash to celebrate an anniversary? Kawasaki Frontale's answer was to push the boat out all the way... into space!

To mark their 20th year, the Tokyo-based side teamed up with the makers of the *Space Brothers* anime series, and came up with this space-themed shirt - complete with stars, a satellite and a honeycomb pattern, which designer Koyama Chu said was intended to replicate the outer wall of a rocket.

It certainly seemed to inspire them to *reach for the stars*, with an *interstellar* result against Ventforet Kofu, the score going *stratospheric*. Sorry... they won 4-0.

Anniversary

Coquitlam Metro-Ford
2014 30th Anniversary Home

Canadian-based Coquitlam Metro-Ford was formed in 2004, following the merger of two local clubs – the Metro-Ford Soccer Club and Coquitlam City Soccer Association – both having been founded in 1984, hence the 30-year anniversary in 2014.

Prior to the merger, the Metro-Ford Soccer Club had won an incredible 22 Provincial Cups in the 18 years they had existed.

CMF is one of British Columbia's largest community sports organisations, offering both recreational and elite soccer programs to over 3,500 players.

Brondby IF
2014 50th Anniversary Home

Initially formed in 1964 as an amateur club, Brondby IF only turned professional in 1977. They've since become one of the most successful Danish clubs, having won the league ten times.

To celebrate their 50th year, they released this beautifully understated shirt with a retro cotton-feel material.

Only a year before, it had looked as though the club may not reach its anniversary, as it had been close to the point of bankruptcy.

Racing Club
2017 1967 Intercontinental Cup Win Special

The Intercontinental Cup once pitted the winners of the European Cup against the Copa Libertadores holders. In 1967, this brought together Scotland's Celtic and Racing Club de Avellaneda of Argentina. Played over two legs, only the result of each match counted, rather than the aggregate number of goals, with a win giving a team two points.

After a win by the home team in both legs, a play-off in neutral Montevideo was required, which Racing Club won 1-0, thus becoming the first club from Argentina to win and become *de facto* world champions.

Fifty years later, the club released this beautiful shirt to celebrate the win.

FC Köln
2018 70th Anniversary Special

Like fellow German side FC Mainz, FC Köln usually release a Karneval shirt in the New Year and, as you'll see later in the book, theirs are some of the best. 2018 marked the club's 70th anniversary, so the usual 'Fastelovend' shirt was eschewed in favour of this commemorative effort.

The shirt itself is reversible with the prime version imitating the shirt the club wore during their first League title win in the 1963-64 season.

The all-white look is enhanced by the manufacturer and sponsor logos rendered in white, whereas the reverse side features the years 1948/2018, created using images from the club's history

Toulouse
2017 80th Anniversary 3rd

If you're going to go retro for your anniversary jersey, this is surely the way to do it, with a full-on vintage lace-up collar, subtle branding and no sponsor!

The shirt also features a specially designed badge, based on the three logos that have been used by the club over eight decades: the coat of arms of the city of Toulouse and a combination of the first club badge from 1937 and the current one.

Interestingly, while it would appear the shirt was a bespoke design especially for Toulouse, it's actually a Joma teamwear template going by the name of 50y. The red version was used as the keeper kit, though oddly with white laces.

CD Leganes
2018-19 90th Anniversary Away

Founded in 1928, the Spanish club celebrated its 90th year by releasing this gorgeous away shirt. Based, strangely, on the colours the club wore a few years after their formation rather than their exact originals, it was worn in the away match against Eibar, which the home side won 1-0.

The beauty of the match shirt was somewhat ruined by the incongruous Betway sponsor. Thankfully, the replicas were sold sponsor free.

If the shirt looks familiar, it would seem to be the same template used by Toulouse for their 80th anniversary.

Universitario
2013 90th Anniversary Away

Two years after the club released what became incorrectly labelled as their 88th anniversary shirt, Universitario turned out in a beautiful set of retro-themed kits to celebrate 90 years.

In true old-skool style, the away is a copy of the home, but in reverse colours, being maroon with red trim. The classic look is completed with Umbro's trademark double diamond tape on the shoulders and a retro-styled collar.

The new crest features 26 stars, each one denoting a Peruvian Championship victory.

Universitario de Deportes
2013 Lolo Fernández 100 Years Special

Originally planned to mark 100 years since the birth of club legend Lolo Fernández (hence the number 9 on the back of replicas), the club's failure to secure his family's permission to use his name and image meant no mention of the player was to be found on the launch of the shirt. Instead, it was officially 'In Honor of our Idols', as detailed inside the neck.

The neat, trimmed collar leads to a neck opening that extends almost all the way down to the abdomen. The club crest is a thick, luxurious, stitched-on patch and the numbers on the back follow this look with contrasting stitching.

It was worn in two matches including a 3-0 win against major rivals, Cristal.

Anniversary

Genoa
2013 'Away Shirt' 100th Anniversary

Look this up and it's almost always listed as Genoa's centenary shirt, but given the club was founded in 1893 and this was released in 2013, it's clearly not that.

So it must therefore be their 120th anniversary shirt? Wrong again.

It is a centenary shirt, but not of the club. It was released to celebrate 100 years since this particular style of away shirt was first worn - in a 4-1 victory over AC Milan... and why not?

Genoa
110th Anniversary Special

In their 110th year, Genoa created this beauty. Made from a heavy, wool-type material, its most distinct feature is neither the deep, lace-up neck nor the minimalist crest with '1893-2003' underneath, nor the lack of any kind of sponsorship.

Instead it's the sleeves, which are neither short nor long, but which finish just below the elbow, a further nod to the historic look of the shirt.

It's unclear if it was ever used in a competitive match.

Hertha Berlin
2017 125th Anniversary Special

I'm a big fan of doing something interesting for commemorative shirts, and Hertha Berlin went down the route of giving fans a choice of different designs for their 125th anniversary outfit.

The six designs were fan made and all featured city landmarks in one form or another. The final choice has a freestyle image of Berlin landmarks such as the Radio Tower, Olympiastadion and Victory Column across the bottom of the shirt, rendered in the club colours of blue and white.

The shirts were worn in a friendly against Liverpool in July 2017. Sadly, there was to be no celebration for Hertha as the visitors ran out 3-0 winners.

VfB Stuttgart
2018-19 125th Anniversary Special

To celebrate the club's 125th year, VfB Stuttgart released this shirt based on the one worn by the club in 1925 when the now-familiar red band was first introduced in a match against Alemania Worms.

Like the 1925 shirt, this has what should be a given on anniversary shirts, a lace-up collar. It also features a version of their 1912 crest depicting three stylised antlers from the House of Württemberg.

While I have a predilection for limited-edition anniversary shirts, I wasn't overly impressed with this one - until I saw the retro numbers and, more specifically, that number 7 with the line through it! SOLD!

Armour

Crusaders FC
2017-18 Away

When your club is named Crusaders, it's surely an obligation to have at least one shirt in your history based on armour.

In 2017, the Northern Irish side did just that with this brilliant away shirt, complete with an all-over chainmail pattern.

Made by Kappa, who have really excelled in the sublimated print game in recent years, it was sadly only worn for one season before the club reverted to a more traditional white shirt.

SC Braga
2019-20 3rd

Picking up the armoured baton for the 2019-20 season, SC Braga of Portugal unveiled this beauty as a third shirt.

Supposedly based on the suits of armour worn by the soldiers of ancient Rome, it's also been speculated that inspiration came from superhero Thor, video game Mortal Kombat and also the rock out of which Braga's stadium is carved.

Whatever the backstory, it's proved unpopular with fans, with an initial poll showing a clear dislike for the unusual design.

AGF Aarhus
2017 City of Culture Special

When the Danish town of Aarhus was named as European Capital of Culture for 2017, the club launched this celebratory one-off shirt, worn in a 2-0 win against Brondby in August of that year.

Limited to 500, the shirt features the Aarhus skyline across the front and, underneath, '2017' replaces the name of the team sponsor, local brewery Ceres.

A nice hidden touch can be found under the collar with the neck featuring blocks of colour forming a rainbow, inspired by Danish-Icelandic artist Olafur Eliasson's Your Rainbow Panorama - a 150-metre-long, rainbow-coloured circular glass walkway on top of ARoS, Aarhus's contemporary art museum.

Athletic Bilbao
2004 UEFA Cup Special

In 2004, Athletic Bilbao qualified for European football for the first time since the turn of the century. To mark the occasion, president Jose Maria Arrante commissioned Basque artist Dario Urzay to create a special strip for the UEFA Cup campaign.

Supposedly inspired by artworks Urzay had seen in the local Guggenheim Museum, he created a design which drew comparisons with paint splats, ketchup and even blood.

The fans despised it and, perhaps mercifully, the team were eliminated in the first knockout stage by Austria Wien.

Bordeaux
2017-18 3rd

It's not a new idea to incorporate into a shirt design images relating to a club's culture or home city, but Bordeaux's attempt is certainly one of the best. Unfortunately, as it was only a third shirt, it didn't see anywhere near as much action as it deserved.

Rendered in blocks of dark blue, pink and purple, the shirt features several of the city's famous landmarks such as the beautiful Place de la Bourse, the Porte d'Aquitaine, an 18th-century city gate, and the Place des Quinconces, one of the largest city squares in Europe.

Marseille
2011-12 Away

Marseille's culture-inspired shirt is one of my all-time favourites. At first glance it appears to be a gold-trimmed, blue shirt with a strange pattern on the front, but closer inspection reveals the print is a collage of images depicting the club's, and also the fans', identity.

It placed 33rd in the Fifty Greatest Football Shirts Ever - a collaboration between The Football Attic, Design Football and John Devlin's True Colours - mainly because I was part of the team who compiled the list and there was no way it wasn't getting in.

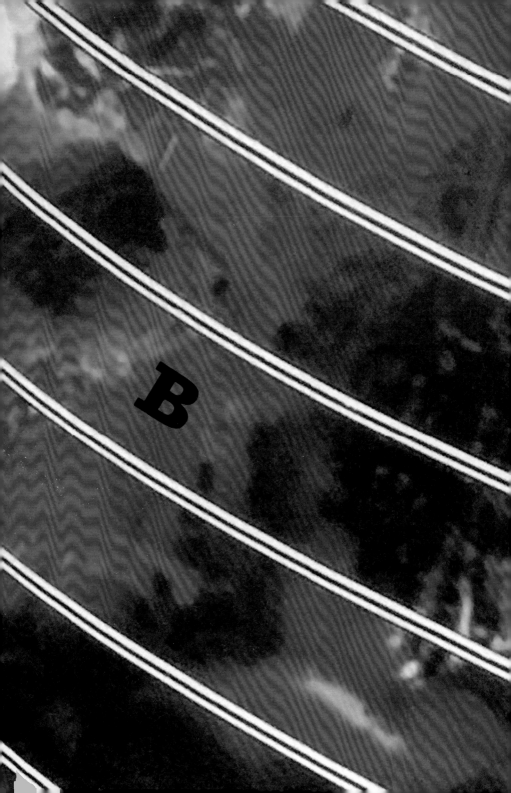

Volga Ulyanovsk
2019 Special Edition

The first day back at school after the summer holidays was always a mixed bag. On the downside, it usually rained, you often had to write a boring essay about what you'd done over the summer and Christmas was months away. On the plus side... erm... you got to learn new stuff.

In Russia, the occasion is known as 'Knowledge Day', which sounds like a lame attempt at a rebrand.

Clearly mimicking a school uniform, the players of Volga Ulyanovsk took to the field looking like First Formers having a playground kickabout - which they did at least win, beating Akron Togliatti 2-0.

Scarborough
1990-91 Home

The laws on football shirt sponsorship can seem rather arbitrary at times. Tobacco products are outright banned, while gambling companies are everywhere. Alcohol is allowed, though not for certain European matches, and particular energy drinks own and rebrand entire clubs.

While the FA banned Kettering Town's 1976 sponsor on the grounds that sponsorship just wasn't a thing back then, by the time Scarborough wore this number in 1990, the concept was fully established. Nevertheless, the FA objected and Black Death was killed off.

Lastly... did no-one care that this shirt was made by a company called Beaver?

Fiorentina
1992-93 Away

One imagines there is quite a robust sign-off process when new kits are created, involving multiple points at which certain design ideas can be changed or even ditched altogether. Seemingly that wasn't the case in 1992 as no-one at Lotto or Fiorentina spotted a rather familiar pattern in the funky design of the new away shirt.

That said, I guess it wasn't exactly on their checklist. Crest? Check. Lotto logo? Check. Sponsor? Check. Symbol of the Third Reich in the design? Er...

Amazingly, it was worn for eight matches before anyone noticed and pulled the shirt from use.

Cameroon
2002 Home

Occasionally, a kit arrives which pushes design down a new path. Spurs' 1991 long shorts; Netherlands' 1988 geometric design; Kappa's close-fitting Kombat.

In 2002, Puma and Cameroon unveiled this 'vest' for the Africa Cup of Nations. While it proved successful for them as they won the tournament, for that year's World Cup, FIFA forced them to attach black sleeves. Got to put those tournament patches somewhere!

Two years later, Cameroon rocked up to the AfCoN in a onesie, which you have to step into and zip up at the shoulders, but FIFA reminded them of their 'shirts and shorts must be separate items of clothing' rule, and that was the end of it.

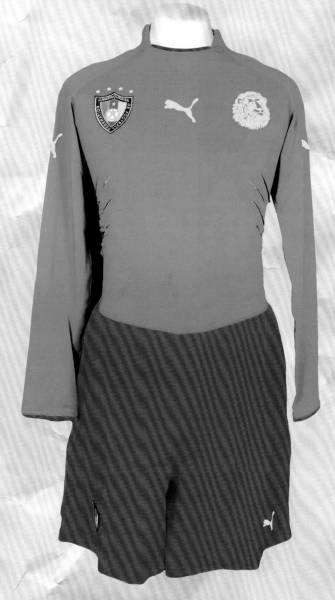

Cameroon
2004 Home

Bedale

Bedale AFC
2016-18 Away

Bedale AFC are a club based in
Yorkshire. They were formed in 1933
and currently play in the North Riding
League Premier Division.

Heck are a sausage manufacturing
company, based in Bedale. They were
founded in 2013 and currently play in
most major supermarkets.

In 2016, Bedale AFC partnered with
Heck to create this sausage-based away
shirt, and the world of football became
all the richer for it.

Bedale AFC
2018-19 GK

When it came to a new raft of kits for
the 18-19 season, Bedale went the
whole... er... hog for the away shirt, as
seen opposite.

This time round they decided to make
the keeper kit food themed too, and
what could be a more British way of
cooking sausages in North Yorkshire
than a BBQ?

Thus this stunning GK shirt was born,
replete with shorts which carried on the
glowing charcoal look. If you ask me,
it's a real banger...

Bedale AFC
2018-19 Away

After the notoriety gained from the previous seasons' sausage-based shirt, Bedale decided to ramp things up for 18-19. Upon the unveiling of this shirt, there was a mixture of horror, joy and disappointment – the latter two caused by the sheer awesomeness of the design and the announcement they were not going to produce replicas due to the admin time spent on the previous shirts.

Thankfully that all changed when Historic Football Shirts offered to produce them, with 25% of proceeds going to Prostate Cancer UK at the club's request.

Meanwhile, the club found itself doing interviews for radio and television across the world, such was the attention it deservedly received.

Bedale

Bedale AFC
2019-20 Away

After the notoriety of the original sausage shirt and the insanity of the hotdog getup, how could Bedale possibly top either of them? What goes perfectly with sausages? Mash, of course! And peas. But wait, where's the gravy? Don't worry, the socks have this covered. Mmmm... gravy socks.

If that wasn't enough for you, just feast your eyes on the naked barbecuing goalkeeper kit opposite. Crack-ing! Sorry...

Sadly, and despite the previous kits, the images of mash (and peas) displeased the FA, who declared it as advertising, despite Heck not selling mash (or peas). They promptly banned the whole lot.

Bedale AFC
2019-20 GK

Bibs

Huddersfield Town
1987-89 Home

There's no doubt that the late 80s brought some crazy kit designs, but while some have become iconic, others have unfortunately found their place in history's bad books.

For years, Huddersfield had played in standard blue and white stripes, but this strayed about as far from tradition as was possible.

One redeeming feature is that it wasn't worn in the club's infamous 10-1 defeat to Man City. The away shirt, which was, had the same bib template, but in yellow with the stripes replaced with black cubes!

St Mirren
1987-89 Home

On 16th May 1987, underdogs Coventry City and St Mirren won the FA and Scottish Cups, respectively. The Buddies did so wearing a sleek Adidas pinstripe / shadow stripe shirt (the modern tribute shirt can be found elsewhere in this book).

When the 87-88 season kicked off, Coventry were now wearing a sky blue version of the classic Hummel 'Denmark 86' shirt, whereas St Mirren ended up in this. Supplied by Matchwinner, it was unsurprisingly loathed by fans - though it is now much sought after.

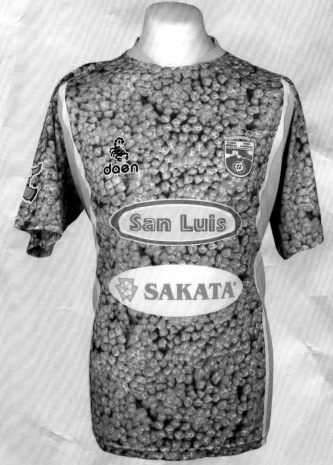

La Hoya Lorca
2013-14 Away

If you want to know the origin of the trend for small clubs releasing controversial shirts for worldwide attention, look no further than the grandfather of the all-over sublimated print, La Hoya Lorca's broccoli kit.

Their first version was released in 2012 and immediately found a place on 'Worst Shirts' lists everywhere. It also ended up in many a shirt collection, such was its notoriety. A marketing master stroke, since repeated ad nauseam by countless imitators.

The team's home shirts at the time, which are rather pedestrian blue and white stripes, also featured a broccoli floret opposite the crest, an idea since dropped.

Camouflage

Club Sport Emelec
2015 3rd

Camouflage patterns on football shirts have become a tad passé in recent years, but this is still quite unique, opting for a modern, digital UCP look, rather than the more common Woodland style.

Based in the Ecuadorian Serie A, SC Emelec were founded in 1929 by an American by the name of George Capwell (whom their ground is named after). He was head of the Electric Company of Ecuador, aka Empresa Eléctrica del Ecuador, from which the club's name is derived.

Partick Thistle
2009-10 Away

Following the more traditional Woodland camo pattern, Partick Thistle mixed things up by rendering their version in shades of pink, black, grey and white.

Their previous away shirt had introduced pink and grey to the colour palette in a simple hooped design, but this took things to another level, much to the chagrin of fans.

While the team are perfectly visible in such a garish outfit, the tonal club crest seems somewhat lost in amongst the chaos.

Centenary

Canada
2012 Special

According to the official blurb, this shirt commemorates "the first official match that Canada played on home soil when they defeated the Americans 1-0 on 27 June, 1925", however, anyone with even a half-decent grasp of arithmetic can see that 1925 + 100 does not equal 2012, so what exactly is it a centenary of?

The Dominion of Canada Football Association was formed in 1912 and joined FIFA the same year.

Part of the Tailored By Umbro range, the shirt has a beautiful minimalist aesthetic. Inside the collar is a soundwave of the national anthem along with the title, "O, Canada" and, on the back, "1912".

C

Corinthians
2010 Special

One of my favourite shirts of all time, it's based on the shirt the Brazilian club first wore back in 1910.

The original shirts were cream coloured, but as soon as the colour faded after washing, they had to buy new shirts. To solve this, they simply decided to adopt white as their new club colour.

The crest is a version of one used on the original shirts, with an intertwined C and P (for Corinthians Paulista), outlined with a gold circle.

EC Taubaté
2014 Special

Bucking the usual trend of anniversary shirts going for a retro feel, Brazilian club Taubaté instead opted for a modern look.

Elements of their past were added to the shirt in the form of the central blue chest band, which houses every different crest they've had throughout their history.

Furthermore, the main badge used on the shirt is their original from 1914, and sits next to a special commemorative shield.

Madureira Esporte Clube
2014-15 Home

Another Brazilian club celebrating their centenary in 2014 was Madureira. As with Taubaté, their shirt was supplied by WA Sport and also featured the same commemorative shield in the centre.

The kit also went for a seemingly modern look, although it was actually identical to one of their earliest shirts.

The club's colours of blue, purple and yellow (the kit had yellow socks) represent, respectively, Fidalgo Madureira Atlético Clube, Madureira Tênis Clube and Imperial Basquete Clube, the three sporting clubs that merged in 1971 to form Madureira Esporte Clube.

Centenary

Athletic Bilbao

1. 1997-98 Home
2. 1997-98 Away
3. 1997-98 Alternative Home

Why have one shirt to celebrate your centenary when you can have three?

For their 97-98 season, Athletic Bilbao did exactly that with the 'celebrating player' motif featured prominently on standard-looking home and away shirts.

They then released the 'lion's head' jersey. Officially designated as a home shirt, it was sadly never worn in a competitive match, the main home shirt being used in all competitions.

A special centenary match against Brazil in May ended in a 1-1 draw.

1

2

3

45

Bologna
2009 Centenary Special

If you're going to go retro for your centenary shirt, why not do it properly and go full-on old skool?

That's exactly what Bologna did in 2009 when they released this beauty with it's plunging, button-up neck and chest pocket. And, in proper limited-edition shirt style, only 1909 replicas were made.

While some shirts inspired by those of yesteryear can be ruined by having multiple matchday sponsors plastered over them, taking away from the overall design, these shirts remained unsullied by both sponsor and even supplier logos when worn in the 3-1 defeat at home to Genoa.

Centenary

Padova
2009-10 Special

Padova were formed on 29th January 1910 and, to mark their 100th year, the club created this outfit made with a fabric of mixed wool and synthetic fibre, specially designed to replicate the look and feel of the first football shirts they wore.

It was worn against Hellas Verona in February 2009 and again in the last home game before the official birthday of 29th January 2010 against Reggina. Both matches ended in 1-0 defeats.

Sadly, the Italian club folded in 2014, but were reborn as Biancoscudati (White Shields) Padova.

Parma
2013 Special

To celebrate their centenary, Parma unveiled this truly beautiful limited-edition shirt, which was not only based on the first shirt they ever wore, but even imitated the material it was made from.

The cream-coloured shirt was manufactured using similar techniques to the original, resulting in a soft woollen material.

It was worn for just one match, against Cagliari, almost 100 years to the day they played their first ever match. The game ended 0-0.

Hajduk Split
2010-11 Home

As with Wisla below, Hajduk was founded by a group of the town's students. They have become one of Croatia's most successful clubs.

The hoops are made up of the lyrics of the club's anthem, 'Bili Su Bili Vrhovi Planin', and the sides of the shirt have a pattern formed from three crowned lions, part of the Dalmatian coat of arms.

To mark the centenary, on 13th February 2011, Hajduk played a friendly game with Slavia Prague in honour of Hajduk's Czech origins. The visitors won 2-0.

Wisla Kraków
2006 Special

Wisla Kraków were formed in 1906 under the name Towarzystwo Sportowe Wisla, by students of the Second Practical School in Kraków, having been inspired by their professor Tadeusz Lopuszanski.

For their centenary in 2006, Umbro released this retro-looking shirt to be worn in a special celebration match against FC Sevilla.

The match ended with a 1-0 victory for the the Polish 'White Star' club, the only goal being scored by Hristu Chiacu in the 58th minute.

Scottish League XI
1990 Home & Away

To celebrate 100 years of the Scottish League, a match against the national side was arranged. Played on August 18th 1990 at Hampden Park, a meagre crowd of 15,085 turned up. And this was back when Hampden, even with a reduced capacity, could accommodate approximately 75,000 people.

Those who did attend saw Aberdeen striker Hans Gillhaus score the only goal via a penalty, after 12 minutes. Unlike replicas, the match shirts carried the logo of DIY chain, B&Q.

Given this was only one match and against a predetermined team, why on earth did they need an away shirt?

49

Che Guevara

Madureira Esporte Clube
2013-14 GK & Home

At a time when third, fourth, tournament-specific and limited-edition shirts seem to be released every other week (and I buy them all - sorry!), it would appear that clubs can find just about any reason to knock up a one-off kit.

In the case of Madureira, they released a special home and goalkeeper kit to celebrate 50 years since Che Guevara paid them a visit.

To raise money back in the 60s, the Brazilian side had embarked on a Western Hemisphere tour, with matches in Colombia, Costa Rica, El Salvador, Mexico and, finally, Cuba. And when they played their final match in Havana, the great revolutionary icon stopped by to meet the team.

Coventry Classics

Coventry City
1975-81 Home

There's no doubting the Admiral
tramline design is one of the most
iconic in shirt history.

Used for a whole raft of teams from
clubs like Dundee to international
sides such as Wales, Belgium and
even Saudi Arabia, this served as
Coventry's home shirt for a whole
six years!

It is of course the brilliant chocolate
brown version that still makes the
headlines, usually for all the wrong
reasons, but this remains a stone-cold
Coventry classic.

Coventry City
1983-86 Away

Yellow had been used before as an
away colour for Coventry, with both
the tramline and Talbot kits having
versions in that colourway, but this
Umbro shirt is an absolute 80s classic.

A V neck with striped trim, pinstripes
and shadow stripes provided a
thoroughly modern look for Coventry.
And it still looked timeless three years
later when Umbro was replaced by
Triple S Sports, who came up with...
the exact same design! OK, not quite -
it had two stripes on the neck and cuff
trim, rather than three. As David
Bowie once said - ch-ch-changes!

Coventry Classics

Coventry City
1986-87 Home

Triple S Sports lasted only a single season at Highfield Road, but what a season!

The design was originally intended to be the same as the previous season's Umbro shirt, just as the away shirt ended up being, but it was instead changed to the now famous blue and white stripes, a design not seen since the 50s.

16th May 1987 cemented this shirt's popularity amongst Coventry fans with the team winning a thrilling FA Cup final, probably still the best day in the club's history.

Coventry City
1987-89 Away

Now Hummel were supplying Coventry's shirts, their Denmark 86-style home kit naturally garnered all the attention, but the away was also another beautiful template from the Hummel catalogue, with a chevron shadow pattern and blue trim.

Continuing with yellow as the away colour, it was first seen in Coventry's return to Wembley in the Charity Shield against Everton that August. While the team looked great, the match couldn't live up to their previous outing and ultimately a Wayne Clarke goal settled things in favour of the Merseysiders.

D

Denim

Diego

Persiba Bantul
2017-18 Away 50th Anniversary

As with camouflage, the denim look is one that's been tried a few times, the most notable being the USA 1994 away shirt, but in terms of replicating the exact look of the jeans fabric, surely none can top this amazing-looking kit from Reds! Sportswear.

This particular jersey was released to celebrate the Indonesian club's 50th anniversary, though there's very little on the shirt denoting it, with only a very subtle "1967-2017" on the back, beneath the collar.

Argentina
2001 'Farewell Diego' Tribute

Despite having ended his playing career four years prior, Maradona played one final match in November 2001 - a testimonial between an Argentina XI and a World XI, which featured stars such as Carlos Valderrama, Hristo Stoichkov, Enzo Francescoli and Eric Cantona.

Maradona scored twice (both penalties) as his side won out 6-4 over the world team.

The shirt appeared to be based on the outgoing Reebok Argentina shirt at the time, despite being made by FILA.

Daensport

1. FC Mena Aguadulce
2017-18 Home

FC Mena Aguadulce are technically a
Fútbol Sala team and their ground
holds only 100 people. The shirt features
a view of the local area at night.

2. AD Caravaca
2015-16 Home

Famous for its Caballos del Vino
(Running of the Wine Horses) festival,
the club are based in Caravaca de la
Cruz and play in Segunda B.

3. Cabezo de Torres
2015-16 Home

Capitalising on the success of La Hoya
Lorca's broccoli shirt, Cabezo de Torres
released their own version, based on
their own local produce, peppers.

1

2

3

Daensport

1. Priego CF
2016-17 Home

Priego Club De Fútbol are based in the Primera Andaluza Córdoba. The local olive oil is regarded as some of the best in the world.

2. CD La Granja
2018-19 Home

Another food-based shirt, this time the judión (butter) beans for which La Granja are famous. The club currently play in Group 8 of the Tercera División.

3. Sporting Club Aguileño
2014-15 Away

In what appears to have been their penultimate season before folding, Sporting Club Aguileño wore shirts featuring psychedelic tomatoes.

1

2

3

Denmark 86

Denmark
1986 World Cup Home & Away

One of the most iconic football shirts of all time, and highly sought after by collectors, the Danish home shirt worn at the 1986 World Cup in Mexico (from which the template gets its name) was, along with the Netherlands 88 shirt, probably responsible for ushering in the crazy designs of the early 90s.

The original shorts that went with the kit followed the same half-and-half design, but in reverse, so the overall look was that of striped quarters. Sadly, FIFA banned the shorts before the World Cup.

At the tournament, despite topping their group, winning all three matches, the Danes crashed out 5-1 to Spain in the Round of 16.

Argentina
1993 'El Jardin De Oscar' Fan Shirt

Owner of the El Jardin De Oscar (Oscar's Garden) fashion brand, Oscar Tubio
was already well known in the football shirt world when, in 1993, he decided to
create a shirt for the fans of several Argentinian clubs.

His aim was to produce a shirt that would enable them to simultaneously show
support for their local club as well as the national side. So Tubio designed a
range of jerseys with each one split diagonally. One half was the shirt above
and the other half reflected the strip of the local club.

Maradona took a liking to them and this full Argentina version was then
released as a shirt in its own right.

Dundee

Dundee
2015-16 'Battle of Loos' 3rd

The Battle of Loos was the most tumultuous of all the British attacks that took place in 1915 on the Western Front during World War I.

Tragically, no less than eight Dundee players were killed during the First World War, including several members of the Black Watch.

This special Black Watch-inspired Battle of Loos remembrance strip includes their tartan, badge and motto 'Nemo Me Impune Lacessit' ('No One Provokes Me With Impunity').

Dundee
2018-19 'SSAFA' 3rd

Following on from the Battle of Loos shirt, Dundee's third jersey for 2018 also had a military theme as the club partnered with SSASA, the Armed Forces Charity.

SSAFA is the UK's oldest military charity and provides financial, practical and emotional support to the Armed Forces community through its network of volunteers across the UK, including the local Dundee branch.

The image across the front of the shirt is that of the cap badge of the Royal Scots Dragoon Guards.

Shirt Stories...

My First Shirt

January 1987. Only seven months after falling in love with football due to the 86 World Cup in Mexico, I was yet to actually own a football shirt. There were several reasons for this. All I had wanted to own to this point was an Argentina home shirt, such was the personal impact of Mexico 86. These were, unsurprisingly, not readily available in England, coming only a few years after the Falklands War. I'll come on to the other reasons shortly but, for now, there I was standing at the tiny chip-shop-counter-style cupboard known as the Coventry City Club Shop at Highfield Road.

Firstly, however, let me give you some background info, for technically this was not my first ever kit. That was a red thing in the guise of Liverpool FC. Half of my family are from that part of the world. And so, before I was even interested in football, my only contact with the sport was via them and this meant occasionally receiving Liverpool-themed gifts.

One Christmas, my brother received a Liverpool kit. I'm not entirely sure it was a genuine replica, but more of a market stall special as it had no badge or manufacturer label and was just all red. This was around 1984, when pinstripes were in. No matter, as we were told it was the official kit and that was all that mattered. A year or so later, it was handed down to me and I proudly ran out in it at school, next to my mate who was also sporting the Liverpool kit, which had pinstripes - inducing confusion in my non-football-following brain. "Mine's the official Liverpool kit," I naively declared. "So's mine," came the response. Brain meltdown. So apparently teams change kits every year or so... Oooh, this football world is full of surprises!

So, picture the scene - a foggy morn, a bolt-hole outlet beloved of 'sell to the public' industrial estate retailers, and an excited pre-birthday 11-year-old gazing at all the merchandise nailed to the wall, which may be a slight exaggeration. Or not...

Sorry, bit more background required here: why was I at the club shop, which, being at the ground itself (none of your town-centre megastores in those days, my friends!) was a fair trek for my non-football-loving parents? Well, despite this being a time before Sports Direct or internet shopping, we did have quite a few sports shops available to us. There was Davies (an Intersport), some other place whose name I can't remember and a small independent sports shop, the type that has 'musty' as its central design theme... the type that also sells school uniforms.

Davies was the place to get your kits though, being a great shop full of proper sporting equipment, including the cricket helmet I yearned for. £125, though! And kits they had! Liverpool (on whom I had turned my back for the glamour

Coventry City
1986-87 Home

of my home town of Coventry City... oops!), Man Utd, Arsenal - even England. And Coventry, of course, what with this being Coventry? No! Not even my hometown shops stocked the blue and white stripes of CCFC.

Back at the club shop: "Do you have the Coventry kit?"

"Yes, we do."

Hmmm... that was easier than I thought. After a while debating what other goodies would constitute my birthday pressie, I ended up with the shirt, shorts and socks... the whole outfit. Interestingly the boys' version of the shorts used a completely different material from the youth's size and given I preferred the boys' ones, I opted for those. I ended up returning them the following week as they were just that bit too small, after all. And this was the 80s, where 'tight' meant circulation problems.

So was I happy? Yes! And no. See, when I obsess about something, I do it full on. My disappointments were as follows. The badge wasn't stitched. In the 80s, no replica badges were stitched (except my England 88 top, but that's yet another story) so I wasn't too disappointed with that, however most badges were generally raised flock affairs. The badge on my shirt was flat. No big deal, but anyway... Secondly - no sponsor. Again, replicas rarely had sponsors on them, though the bigger teams (those available in Intersport) did. Again, not a major issue, but it bugged me a little. Yes, perhaps I should get a life...

What's most surprising when I look at that kit now (replete with a red number 7 made from some old pyjamas that I stitched on myself), is how tiny it is. It's like a doll's shirt. OK, so I was a child and now both my age and waist size are the wrong side of 40, but it's still shockingly small. It's also aged very well. The badge does have bits missing from repeated wearing / washing and the Triple S Sports logo is similarly jaded, but the colours are still as vibrant as when I first got it.

Of course, Coventry went on to win the FA Cup in this shirt and I not only took great pride in following my home team, but also got called a glory-hunter for doing so!

Unsurprisingly, this is one of the Coventry fans' favourite kits, but not mine. My personal favourite was to come the following season as we moved into the world of 'name brand' kit manufacturers. The gloriousness that was the Hummel 'Denmark 86'-style kit - one which garners mixed reactions amongst CCFC fans.

And finally the replicas carried the sponsor's name, too - that well-known brand, Granada Bingo. A Coventry fan's lot can be quite a burden!

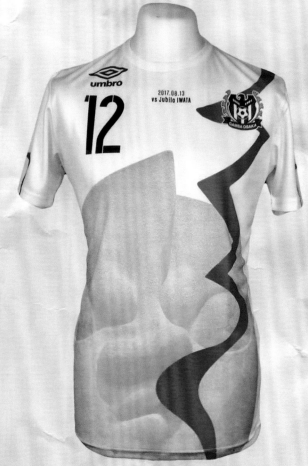

Gamba Osaka
2017 Expo Fan Shirt

For their 2017 Gamba Expo match, the Osaka team took to the field in shirts with imagery pertaining to the Banpaku Memorial Park's Tower of the Sun monument, designed by Taro Okamoto in 1970 for the original Gamba Expo. The face on the front is meant to represent the present.

Replica versions were on sale featuring a raised crest and fewer sponsors on the back, but this is the fan version which was only given to ticket holders at the game against Jubilo Iwata on August 13th.

As with most 'fan' shirts in Japan, it has the number 12 on the back to represent the supporter - the '12th man'.

Gamba Osaka
2018 Gamba Expo Special

While J.League shirts have a reputation for consistently being amongst the most crazy out there, one featuring sharks, jellyfish, trilobites and dinosaurs surely has to be next level. There is, however, a logical reason for it all.

Expo 70, the first in Asia, was held in Osaka and featured a 230-metre structure known as the Tower of the Sun. The interior featured a 'tree of life' with the aforementioned creatures to the fore. Over time the tower fell into disrepair, but in 2016 a campaign to restore it began.

To celebrate Expo 2018, Gamba Osaka released this wondrous outfit depicting the interior of the revived tower, worn in a 2-0 defeat to Sanfrecce Hiroshima.

Brazil
2004 FIFA Centenary Match Home & GK

To celebrate its 100th anniversary, FIFA organised a match between the World Cup holders of the time, Brazil, and European champions, France.

For the game, France wore a replica of the kit from their first match in 1904, consisting of blue, collared shirts, long cream shorts with a belt, and red socks. Brazil's outfit, above, was based on one worn in 1914, combined with white shorts and blue socks.

The match, which ended in a somewhat predictable 0-0 draw, took place in May 2004, only a month before the European Championships - so, had FIFA been formed later in the year, Brazil would have faced off against Greece.

Corinthians
2018-19 3rd

São Paulo-based Corinthians released this special kit to mark 30 years since hometown Formula One legend, Ayrton Senna, won his first world title.

The design is inspired by the Lotus he drove in 1985 and 1986, so in effect it's actually in the colours of tobacco brand John Player Special.

The chest bands are made up of 41 thin gold lines, each of which represents one of Senna's Grand Prix victories.

Sadly, the kit wasn't enough to inspire the team to win as they wound up on the wrong side of a 3-0 defeat to Flamengo.

Fractals

Kilwinning Rangers
2017-18 Home

Ask any fan about football shirts and one of the most common complaints you'll hear is about the price, with player-spec versions often costing nearly £100.

To combat this, Ayrshire-based Kilwinning Rangers made the bold step of releasing a complete kit of shirt, shorts and socks, all for £25!

Given how much smaller clubs rely on cash to survive, such a move to put their fans first should be wholly applauded and serve as an example to larger clubs everywhere.

Wycombe Wanderers
2017-18 GK

While goalkeeper shirts have always been distinct from the outfield jerseys, the early 90s trend for crazy designs stuck around between the sticks long after it had died out upfield. It became almost expected that the guy with the gloves would be wearing something pretty hideous.

Wycombe decided to take this to the extreme and deliberately created this kaleidoscopic fractal-inspired shirt to be as off-putting to the opposition as possible, apparently designed to make the keeper appear larger to incoming strikers... or maybe just blind them.

CD Pinzón
2015-16 Home & Away

Fruit

After watching La Hoya Lorca gain worldwide attention with its broccoli-based shirt, other small clubs took note and a host of garish designs ensued (see 'Daensport').

Based in the province of Huelva, Spanish side CD Pinzón went down the same path as their compatriots and switched out their usual home and away jerseys for ones representing the area's local produce of strawberries and blueberries.

While the kits did indeed get some press, they failed to catch on like their forebears, and they now appear to have dropped the idea – which seems a shame as they're surely one of the best of their kind.

G

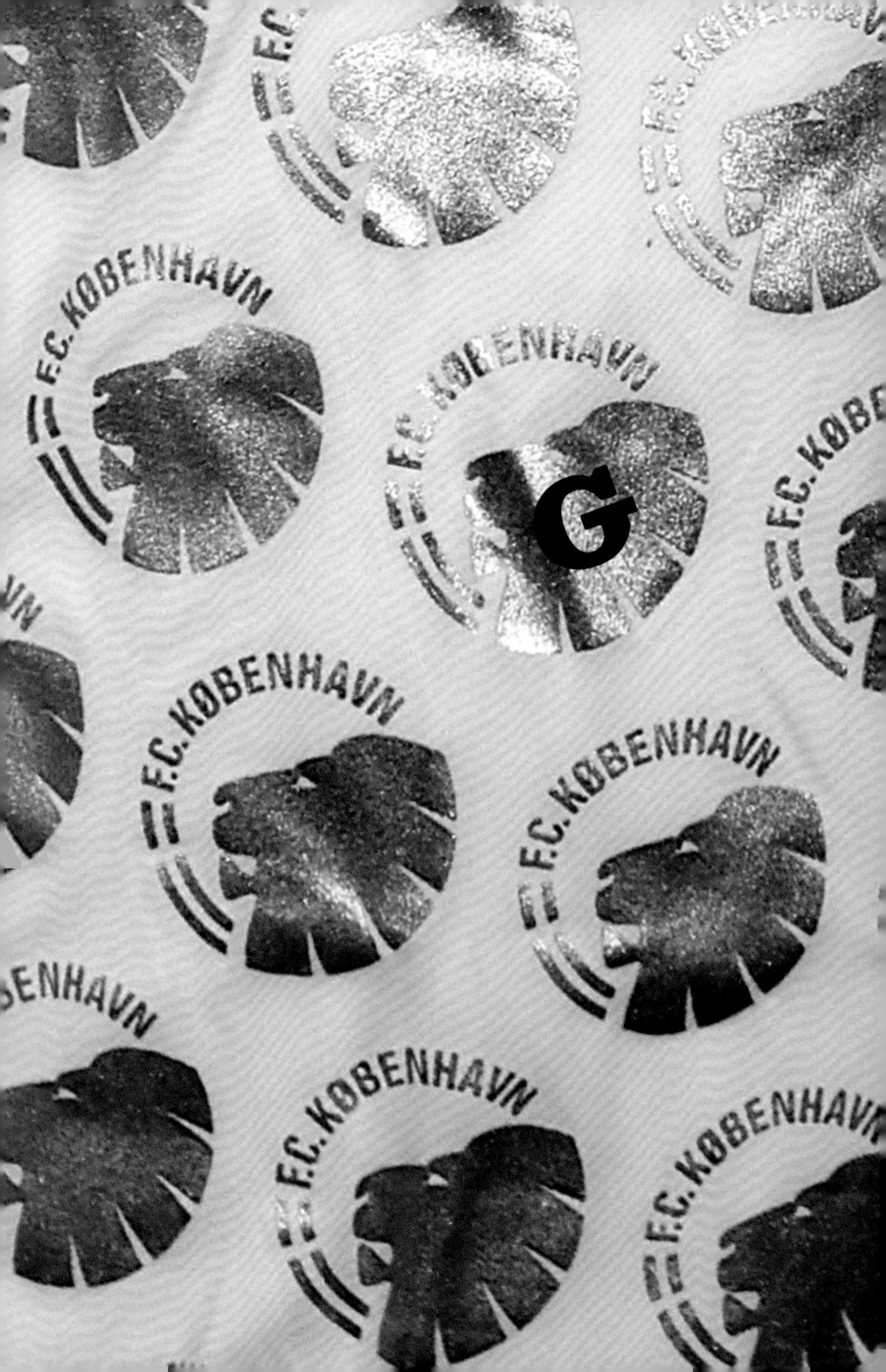

Lewes FC
2019-20 Special Edition Home

At the time of writing, 27 of the 44 teams in the top two divisions in England have a gambling company as their main sponsor.

A recently published study showed that 5% of problem gamblers attempted suicide in the last year - eight times the rate for the general population.

Determined to take a stand, Lewes FC proudly wore the logo of 'Gambling with Lives', a charity set up to "to support families who have been bereaved by gambling related suicides; and to raise awareness amongst gamblers, their families and friends, and health professionals of the dangerous effects of gambling on mental health and the high suicide risk."

Coventry City
1987-89 Home

7th January 1989 is a date etched into most Coventry and Sutton fans' minds, albeit for very different reasons. Just 18 months after lifting the trophy in one of the best FA Cup finals ever, Coventry were drawn against non-league Sutton United for their first match of the 1989 Cup campaign. Fourth round, here we come!

By 4:50pm, both sides had claimed a place in Cup history, with only the Gander Green Lane side celebrating. Call me twisted, but ever since then I'd wanted to own that Sutton shirt.

As for the best ever Coventry shirt, it surely deserves a better legacy than this!

Sutton United
1987-89 Home

Gold

Grounds

Copenhagen
2007 Special

To celebrate the Danish club's 2006-07 Superliga win, Kappa released this commemorative shirt.

The design is similar to the jerseys used in the following season's European Champions League, where they reached the group stage for the first time, being white with gold collar.

The other key difference, of course, is the gold club crests which completely cover the rest of the shirt.

It was never actually worn in a match.

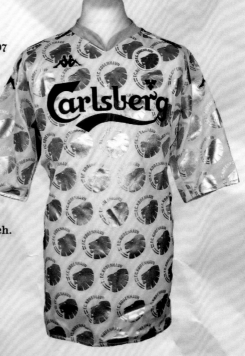

Heart of Midlothian
2016-17 Special Home

At the end of the 2016-17 season, Hearts began demolition of the 103-year-old main stand, designed by renowned football ground architect, Archibald Leitch

To mark the stand's passing, the club released limited-edition versions of the home and away shirt featuring a gold embroidered image of the stand.

Despite Leitch's work once dominating football grounds up and down Britain, only the main stand at Craven Cottage and the façade of the main stand at Ibrox now remain.

78

River Plate
2013-14 3rd

Club Atlético River Plate was founded in 1901, but they didn't move into their current home until 1938, having played at four different stadiums in the intervening 37 years.

At the time, the club was known as Los Millonarios, or The Millionaires, due to purchasing several players at inflated prices.

This shirt was released to celebrate 75 years at Estadio Monumental, which was officially renamed Estadio Antonio Vespucio Liberti in 1986.

CA Independiente
2017 Special

Independiente released this shirt to celebrate the completion of the reconstruction of their stadium, Estadio Libertadores de América, depicted on the front in relief.

The stadium was closed in December 2006 and was demolished the following year. The rebuilt stadium was inaugurated on October 28, 2009, in a match against Colón de Santa Fe, however the stadium had only been 60% finished.

It took another seven years for the rest of the stadium to be completed.

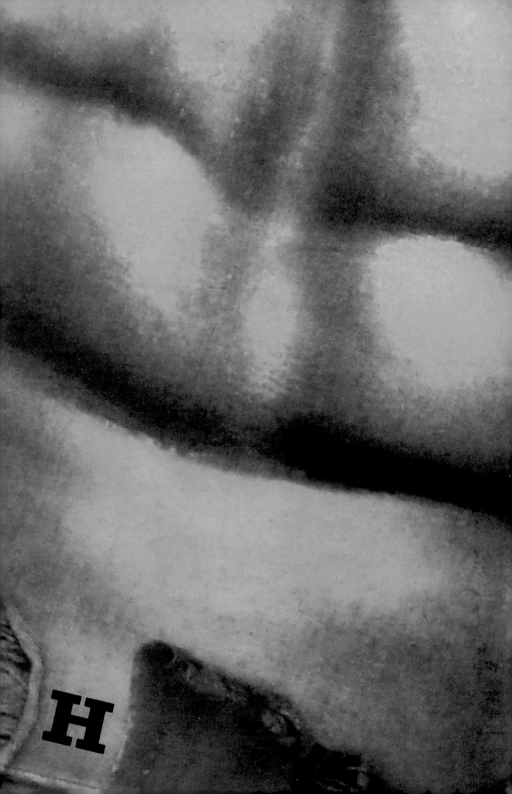

H

Providence City FC
2019-20 HAMR Special Edition

Yet another small team coming up with a wacky shirt, and this time from over the pond in America. Providence City FC are a US non-league side, currently competing in the Bay State Soccer League.

The shark motif is from their main sponsor, Revival Brewing Company, and their HAMR Oceanic State Pale Ale. According to the marketing spiel, it's "a brew with a bite. The shining sun colouring glides by with a hop aroma that's stubbornly bold."

I'm no beer fan, but sharks are ace so this shirt rools - a feeling shared amongst fans and collectors alike as the shirt sold out instantly.

CD Guijuelo
2015-16 Away

After the worldwide attention La Hoya Lorca's broccoli shirt received, it wasn't long before other Spanish clubs leapt on the bandwagon, and who better to deliver the goods than the original's creator, Daensport.

In 2015, fellow Segunda B side, CD Guijuelo, decided to follow the same path and, being based in the Salamanca region of Spain, which is famous for its ham, this beauty / monstrosity was born.

If you ever wonder about the effectiveness of kits like these, bear in mind that CD Guijuelo have been talked about worldwide, but their home ground, the Estadio Municipal de Guijuelo, holds a grand total of 1,500 people.

Half & Half
Hashtag

CD Guijuelo
2016-17 Copa Del Rey Special

If you thought their ham shirt was bad, get a load of this!

Half-and-half shirts are generally reviled by football fans, so why does this exist?

In the 2016-17 season, CD Guijuelo reached the final phase of the Copa Del Rey, where they were drawn against Atlético Madrid, and this was created to celebrate. Unsurprisingly, it wasn't actually used in either match.

Unfortunately for the club, but maybe not for football, they went no further, beaten 10-1 on aggregate.

Hashtag United
2017-18 Home

Hashtag United Football Club was formed in March 2016 by Spencer Owen, a football YouTuber who went by the name Spencer FC.

Initially, they played five-, seven- and 11-a-side exhibition matches, which they uploaded to YouTube.

In 2018, the club joined the English football league system, in the Eastern Senior League.

They went on to win the Division One South title, earning promotion to the Essex Senior League.

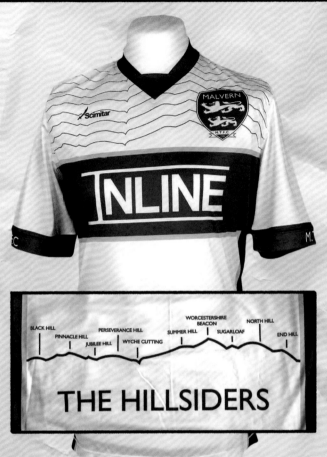

Malvern Town
2018-19 Away

The club was established in 1946 as Barnards Green Football Club, since which time they have found themselves moving up and down the football pyramid on a frequent basis.

They currently play in Division One West of the Hellenic League, having been transferred there at the end of the 2018-19 season from the West Midlands (Regional) League.

The top of the shirt features several lines which depict the skyline of the nearby Malvern Hills. The back of the shirt goes even further and includes the names of the hills themselves, a really nice touch for a local side.

Atlético Astorga
2017 Play-off Special Home & GK

Atlético Astorga play in Group 8 (Castile and León) of the Tercera División, the fourth tier of Spanish league football. They finished the 16-17 season in second place, earning them a spot in the play-offs.

To motivate the team, the club, who play in green, released this Incredible Hulk-inspired home shirt. What really makes the kit is the shorts, with their ripped denim look, and the green socks. All it needs is a green baselayer to top it off!

How much it helped is hard to say. They did make it through to the final round, but lost on away goals to Vitoria.

I

Peña Deportiva Ibiza
2018-19 3rd

Think 'Ibiza' and immediately one tends to picture... well, maybe pissed-up tourists falling over in the street and holiday reps with trays of cheap sour shots... but also nightclubs.

Peña Deportiva are based on the island of Ibiza, the spiritual home of clubbing, so the only surprise about this shirt's existence is that it's taken this long to produce a raver-friendly football shirt.

The last few years have seen Hummel making waves in the all-over print, and this beauty features a 'Karma DJ', also referred to a 'peaceful disco Buddha' on the front, and an image of Ibiza town's skyline on the reverse.

Imitation

Brunei DPMM
2014 Away

With great ideas, there will always be copycats, so it should be no surprise that some of the most iconic designs in football shirt history have also been, shall we say, 'borrowed'?

First up, Duli Pengiran Muda Mahkota Football Club (His Royal Highness the Crown Prince of Brunei Football Club) and their Lotto version of Arsenal's infamous 'bruised banana' Adidas shirt from the 90s.

Interestingly, Portsmouth had a near-identical Influence shirt the same season as Arsenal, so who exactly copied whom?

Geylang International
2015 Away

I've always been surprised that no-one ever seems to have re-used Admiral's awesome tramline design, not even Admiral themselves, barring a York City shirt in the late 90s. Then I found this away shirt from Singapore-based Geylang International.

Nearly identical to Coventry's tramline kit of the early 80s, the design even continues on to the shorts, as did the original.

Perhaps one of the best things about this whole getup is the name of the manufacturer - Dreamatron. So 80s!

Imitation

Adidas Ipswich Template
Napoli Club Bolzano

1988 W.Ger Template
Manufactured by ABM / Ennerre

1988 saw the birth of two of the best
football shirt designs of all time with
the West Germany 'ribbon' shirt and
the Netherlands' geometric pattern.

As with all great designs, it was only a
matter of time before others jumped on
the bandwagon and Italy seems to have
spearheaded the way with ABM and
Ennerre creating their own versions of
the ribbon design. The latter reversed
the stripes, foreshadowing Germany's
own re-interpretation for their 2018
World Cup shirt.

Virma Sportswear created this
interpretation of the Ipswich template
for Italian club, Napoli Club Bolzano.

Wrexham AFC
1989-90 Away

As you'll see in a few pages' time, Denmark's classic shirt from 1986 was available in multiple colourways, but it also got copied... a lot!

While this Wrexham version, made by Spall, may not have the raglan sleeves of the original, it's otherwise a carbon copy, albeit with a rather garish green and yellow colour scheme.

Given that Wrexham were languishing in Division Four at the time, it's hardly surprising this shirt isn't that well known, though they did finish runners-up in the Welsh Cup this season. As the home side, however, they took to the field in their usual red.

Imitation

Hummel Mexico Template
Manufactured by Saller

Yet more Denmark 86 copies, this time by German manufacturer, Saller - though you'd never know to look at them, as they have no external branding whatsoever. It's only when you look at the neck label that you have any clue who makes them.

Though they may look the same as the Hummel shirts, the one key difference is the solid panel on the right is just that - a block of plain, unpatterned colour which takes the place of the familiar two-tone stripes from the wonderful Mexico template.

Copies like these give an insight into what could have been for certain teams. Imagine Fiorentina wearing that purple number!

Imitation

Hummel Mexico Template
Manufactured by Meyba / ABM

Further proof of how widely this particular template was copied comes with the news of two more manufacturers' own DIY versions.

Meyba, famous for Barcelona's classic 1980s shirts, emulate the Hummel style, though replacing the usual chevrons down the sleeve with their own logo, which doesn't quite work. It seems a shame they never adopted this template for Barca as the version shown here by ABM would have been truly amazing.

The Italian sportswear supplier, making yet another appearance in this section, actually supplied a truly awesome version of this design to Palermo in pink and black!

Deportivo Guadalajara
2015-16 Home

While some clubs release a one-match special or a limited-edition third shirt to support good causes, Deportivo Guadalajara nailed their colours firmly to the mast by emblazoning their home shirt with a bold rainbow right down the middle, in support of the LGBT movement.

As part of Hummel's Changing the World Through Sport initiative, 5% of the profits from the sale of the shirts went directly to the CD Guadalajara Foundation for eliminating stigma and prejudice in sport.

Rayo Vallecano
2015-16 Away

Rayo Vallecano's away shirt that year also featured a rainbow, though each colour stood for a different organisation the club donated money to, while the rainbow as a whole represented LGBT causes.

The red stripe is for those tackling cancer, orange is for those fighting for the integration of disabled people, yellow is for 'those who have lost hope', green is for people striving to protect the environment, blue is for those fighting against child abuse, while pink is for the victims of domestic violence.

Altrincham
2018-19 Football v Homophobia Special

Many clubs hold events to show support for the LGBT+ community, the most notable being the Rainbow Laces campaign where footballers swap their usual laces for rainbow-coloured ones.

Altrincham decided to go much further for Football v Homophobia's Month of Action and LGBT History Month, and played their match against Bradford Park Avenue in kits designed around the LGBT flag. The club's regular sponsors gave up the front of the shirt for the Football v Homophobia logo.

Sales of the matchworn shirts raised £2,500, which went towards a campaign to finance a major refurbishment of Manchester's LGBT+ centre.

Whitehawk FC
2019-20 'Football United' Special

On 4th August 2019, Whitehawk Football Club - Brighton's second biggest football club - hosted 'Football United'.

The match pitted a team of ex-Premier League Stars, including ex-Aston Villa midfielder Lee Hendrie and former Manchester United winger Keith Gillespie, against 'Rainbow Rovers', a team of LGBTQ+ players, activists and supporters.

The Rainbow Rovers kit was designed by International Turner Prize Artist David Shrigley OBE. The squiggly lines aren't just fancy design - they're a map of the local area with Whitehawk's TerraPura Ground depicted at the bottom right on the back of the shirt.

Inside Out

A popular method of celebrating anniversaries in the late 2000s was the reversible shirt.

Usually combining a standard-looking jersey, which would be used in a match, with a collage-based all-over print on the reverse side, generally only found on the replicas.

1. St Pauli
2010-11 Centenary Home

While the inside features imagery representing the club, it was the gorgeous copper side which saw action, against Bayern Munich in May 2011.

Sadly, an 8-1 defeat somewhat took the shine off the day as it confirmed St Pauli's relegation from the Bundesliga.

1

2. 1860 Munich
2010 150th Anniversary

The standard side featured the club's original gold and green colours and was worn in a 2-1 win against St Pauli in March 2010.

The reverse side features a blue collage featuring several players from the club's history.

3. Fenerbahce
2006-07 Centenary Home

This reversible shirt was actually a combination of two separate strips.

The striped jersey was worn as the home shirt when Fenerbahce finished champions of the Super Lig, whereas the gold version was worn for their Uefa Cup matches.

2

3

Clapton CFC

2018-19 3rd

Commemorating the 80th anniversary of the end of the Spanish Civil War, this shirt was inspired by the flag of the Spanish Republic, adorned with the three-pointed star of the International Brigades, who travelled to Spain to help the fight against the fascist General Franco.

Clapton Community FC initially expected to sell around 250 shirts, but after word got round on social media they became inundated with requests.

By the time they stopped taking orders, they'd sold approximately 11,500 away shirts with around 5,500 going to Spain and 4,500 sold within the UK, helping raise money for both the club and the International Brigade Memorial Trust.

USA
1988 Away

While the most famous incarnation of this shirt (Netherlands 88) can be found elsewhere in this book, the design was a very common Adidas template, with the rather mundane name of Ipswich!

As can be seen overleaf, it was popular among lower-league sides across Europe – though a blue version was also worn by mighty Argentina in a friendly against Linfield in the run-up to the 1990 World Cup.

The USA away shirt doesn't seem to have ever been worn in a match, and is also notable as the pattern appears upside-down.

USSR
1988-89 Home

Despite making its debut at the same tournament as the Netherlands version, this is perhaps the third best-known colourway of this template, with the West Germany 1990 away shirt beating it to second place.

Maybe if the USSR had got to wear their home shirt for more than one match at Euro 88, theirs may have had a more lasting legacy, although the bright orange of the Dutch and turquoise-green of West Germany were always going to stay in the memory more than the simple red of the Soviet jersey.

Ipswich

I

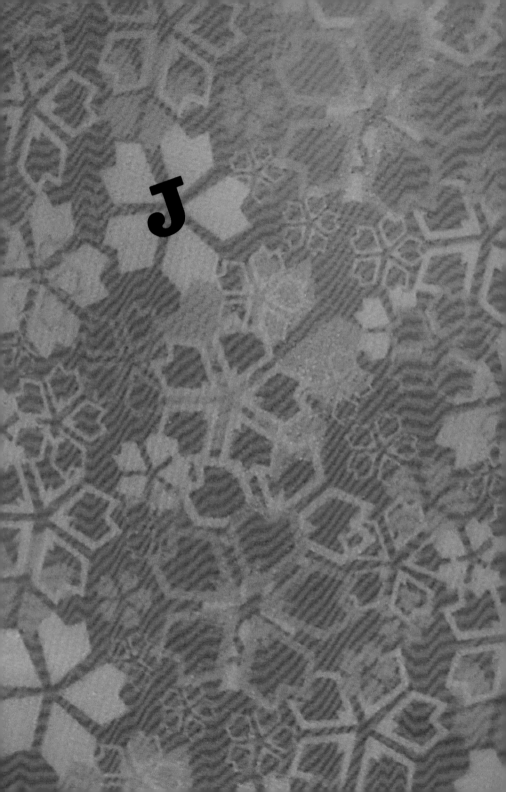

Jack Sparrow

Molinos El Pirata
2018 Home

If the character on the club crest looks familiar, that's because it is indeed Johnny Depp as Captain Jack Sparrow from the *Pirates of the Caribbean* films. If you're wondering how the Peruvian club could afford to license such an image, the answer is... they didn't.

Inevitably, to avoid any possible copyright infringement, they decided to change it, and so replaced Mr Depp with a generic pirate image.

Unfortunately, the one they chose was itself copyrighted, so they then had to change it once more. They eventually settled on a look-alike of the original Jack Sparrow.

Cerezo Osaka
2015 Kincho Stadium 5th Anniversary Home

Cerezo Osaka play the majority of their games at the Nagai Ball Stadium, also known as 'Kincho Stadium' after the corporate sponsors of the ground.

In 2010, the first phase of much-needed renovation was completed, and five years later they released a limited-edition shirt to celebrate the fifth anniversary of said work, because... well, why not?

The design mixes the team's usual pink, derived from the cherry blossom flowers the club's name is based on, and light blue, reminiscent of the 1994-96 shirt, in which they won the JFL and attained promotion to the J.League. It was worn on August 8th, in a 1-1 draw with JEF United.

Tokyo Verdy
1993-95 Home

Formed in 1969 as Yomiuri FC, named after the Yomiuri media conglomerate which created the club.

The club is now known by its full name of Tokyo Verdy 1969 Football Club, although when this shirt was issued, they went by the name of Verdy Kawasaki, as the club were based in the city. It wasn't until 2001 that they moved back to Tokyo.

The Verdy part of the name stems from the Portuguese 'verde', meaning 'green', and is of course derived from the colour of their jerseys, which have to be one of the most recognisable of all J.League shirts.

Newcastle Jets
2015-16, 2016-17 & 2018-19 RAAF Special Editions

The Australian A-League side are based 20 kilometres away from the Williamtown Royal Australian Air Force Base, which is Australia's main fighter-pilot training facility, hence the three F/A-18 Hornets on the Newcastle Jets badge.

Since 2015, the club has held a special annual RAAF day, where they give away thousands of tickets to both military and civilian staff at the base, and the team wear special Air Force-themed shirts.

Thankfully the shirts are usually kept sponsor free, allowing the all-over prints to get the attention they deserve.

K

Karneval

FC Köln

Since 2013, FC Cologne have released a special kit to celebrate the city's annual carnival, known locally as 'Fastelovend'.

The shirts incorporate elements representing the city and the carnival itself, such as the Cologne coat of arms, the 'Narrenkappe' (the traditional headgear worn during the Carnival) and Cologne Cathedral.

They are usually styled similar to clothes worn during the celebrations, with the 2015-16 shirt perhaps being the most memorable.

This year's shirt features a map of Cologne and its nine boroughs.

1. 2013-14

2. 2014-15

3. 2015-16 GK

1

2

3

FC Köln

2015-16 Karneval Special Edition

2019-20 GK

2017-18

2018-19

FC Köln
Karneval Special Edition

FC Köln
2019-20 Karneval Special Edition

Karneval

Mainz 05

Carnival season in Mainz is known as 'Fastnacht'. Like Cologne's big knees-up, it traditionally begins on November 11th at 11:11 am and continues through to Ash Wednesday, when the event comes to its climax.

Their initial shirts were mostly traditional, only embellished with flashes derived from the French flag of blue, white and red as well as yellow; but in the last few years the club have embraced the direction set by others with some striking designs.

While the latest continues that trend, it's the 2019 shirt which truly stands out by making the four colours not just trim, but the basis of the entire design.

1. 2016-17

2. 2017-18

3. 2019-20

1

2

3

Mainz 05
2018-19 Karneval Special Edition

Shirt Stories...

Shirts That Never Were

Argentina
'1996-97 Home' & '1988 Home'

As a collector who cares about the details, nothing irks me more than seeing shirts labelled as something they're obviously (to me, anyway) not. More often that not, it's just a case of innocent mistakes born of ignorance and probably having a life. Other times, it's almost like an urban legend, where every mention of a particular shirt will tell you that it's a certain thing, when it actually isn't.

For years, I've been seeing this Argentina shirt all over the internet, from eBay to proper retailers, and it's usually described as the 96-97 home shirt. I know this to be inaccurate as I'm a complete nerd when it comes to Argentina kits, and I happen to know that between World Cups 94 and 98 they had only one other style of shirt – although it did appear in about four different versions!

A few years ago, I stumbled upon a website bursting with Argentina Kit Nerd Porn (enunabaldosa.com), and what did I happen to find but that 96-97 shirt! A quick use of Google Translate, and at last I had an answer – and I was right! It never was an official AFA shirt! It turns out it was a proposal Adidas put forward for the 1994 kit, but which was rejected due to the navy pinstripes, the AFA insisting there would be no colour other than the light blue and white on the shirt. Four years later, they finally allowed black detailing on the shirts worn at World Cup 98.

The final twist in this tale is that the shirt *was* actually released as a replica for sale, as it shows up in some adverts prior to USA 94, which would explain why there are so many of them around.

So, what of the '1988' shirt? From 1980 to 1990, Argentina's shirts were supplied by French company Le Coq Sportif, so the fact the '1988 Home' shirt is made by Adidas should ring alarm bells. That said, Adidas did indeed supply shirts for Argentina in 1988, but only for the Olympics... so it's the Olympics shirt, right? No. Those were V necked and, as with other Olympic football shirts, featured the Argentina flag with the Olympic rings in place of the crest.

The crest on this shirt is also the one last used in the late 70s – and therein lies the answer. This wasn't a match shirt or even a replica. The shirt *is* from 1988, but it's actually a tribute jersey released to mark ten years since Argentina won the 1978 World Cup.

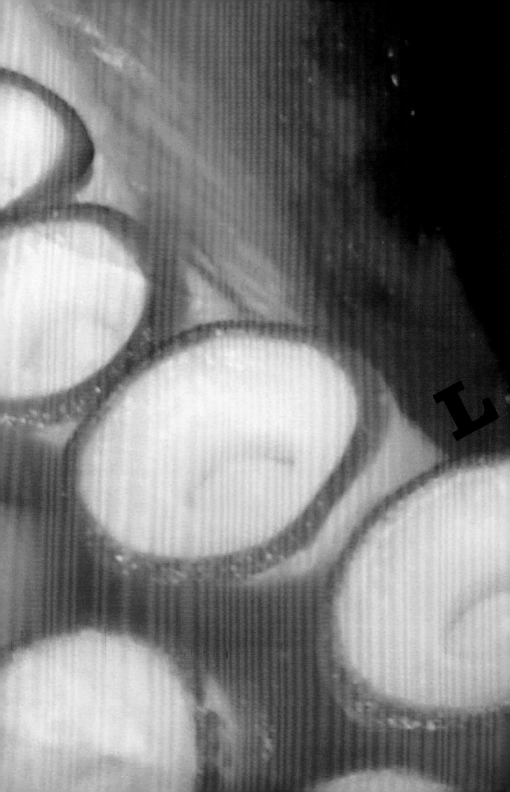

Lazi-oh!

Holyhead Town
2019-20 Home & Away

In 1982, SS Lazio took to the field in a stunning new shirt design featuring a large eagle emblem with wings spreading across the chest. They revived the concept for their 115th anniversary and it's become a modern classic.

Welsh club Holyhead Town have no connection to Lazio, but the club secretary loved the design so much, he conceived this rather excellent appropriation of the idea.

The club are known as the Harbourmen, and the ship represents the influx of ferry and freight traffic to the port in the 50s and 60s, when the non-leaguers once reached as far as the quarter-final of the Welsh Cup.

117

FC Yenisey Krasnoyarsk
2018-19 Special Edition Home

When FC Yenisey Krasnoyarsk gained promotion to the Russian Premier League, it was announced they would wear two special kits for their inaugural season. These were the shirt shown above and its away counterpart, which featured a garish artist's interpretation of the city's architecture, including the cathedral and the railway bridge across the Yenesei River – although the bridge looked unfortunately like a pair of brown Y-Fronts.

Alas, neither shirt was worn in the unsuccessful campaign. Shirt suppliers Joma refused to let the team wear the non-Joma-produced home, and the away appears never to have gone into production. As some small consolation, the home shirt did see some match action when it was worn by the reserves.

Llanfairpwll FC
2019-20 Home

Clwb Pêl Droed Llanfairpwllgwyngyllgogerychwyrndrobwllllantysiliogogogoch, thankfully usually shortened to Llanfairpwll FC, is the local side in the infamous Welsh town with the longest name in Europe. Now all I need is a football shirt from the hill in New Zealand with 85 letters (Llanfairpwll has 58).

The shirt is inspired by the Arsenal design of 95-96 and similarly has the club name along the bottom, though of course this one stretches all the way around the entire jersey.

It also features a sleeve tribute to their former striker, Henry Esin, aka Romeo, who was tragically killed in 2017.

CD Lugo

2014-15 'Authentic Collection' Home

The expected media furore duly ensued when Spanish side CD Lugo released their 2014-15 kits, featuring beer and an octopus. There was one slight issue with the stories, however.

These were not that season's match shirts but instead part of an 'Authentic Collection' the club released, which were only worn for pre-season matches.

The beer design was in honour of the club's shirt sponsor, the Spanish brewery and lager brand, Estrella Galicia. The octopus was inspired by the Galician seafood speciality, *polbo á feira*, which is served during the Festa de San Froilan in Lugo, celebrating the patron saint of the city.

CD Lugo
2014-15 'Authentic Collection' GK

M

Arsenal
2014 '20 Years of Nike' Special

Mashup shirts seem to have become a bit of a mainstream thing in the last few years, with many big clubs including Barcelona and Manchester City releasing official versions, and Internazionale even wearing theirs in the Milan derby.

The Arsenal one was the first, but it was no money-making scheme as they were never sold. Only two were ever made, and mine is an unofficial copy. They were created to celebrate 20 years of Nike at Arsenal, just before the club switched to Puma.

Doncaster Rovers
2018-19 3rd

Teaming up with NHS Doncaster CCG, the club held a competition for young people to design a third shirt to raise money for the mental health charity dealing with suicide, Campaign Against Living Miserably (CALM).

The winner was Nate Nisar, who explained his idea: "I went with the triangles because I wanted to choose a retro design, with the colours representing emotions. People with mental health issues can be feeling lots of different emotions, represented by the variety of different colours."

Mexico

As with the Netherlands' 88 'Ipswich' template, Denmark's iconic shirt from the 1986 World Cup was also an 'off-the-shelf' pattern adopted by clubs up and down leagues across the globe.

Known as 'Mexico', it was used by notable teams such as Coventry, Southampton and Hellas Verona as well as those here, while also being worn in a wide range of colours by a host of lower-league teams across Europe, shown opposite.

1. Feyenoord
1987-89 Home

2. Aston Villa
1987-89 Home

3. Aston Villa
1987-89 Away

4. Pisa
1988-90 Home

1

2

3

4

FutBol CluB de Roast
2019-20 'Roast' Shirt

FC Roast were founded in 2015 as a five-a-side club but, by billing themselves as an Irish Heritage team, have grown hugely in the intervening years. They now have the primary mission of becoming the biggest Irish side in London.

The hand-drawn club badge consists of a cud-chewing cow, which seems to be dispensing its Guinness milk directly into a pint glass. The 'O' in Roast is replaced with a potato. One would assume a roast (though it appears to be raw).

While the Roasts usually play in green and white hoops, they released this special 'Roast' jersey in 2019, created by the up-and-coming American shirt manufacturers, Icarus FC.

Volga Ulyanovsk
2019 Lenin 149 Special Edition

Viewed by some as a hero of socialism and the working class and by others as the head of an authoritarian regime responsible for political oppression and mass killings, Vladimir Ilyich Ulyanov - better known as Lenin - remains a divisive figure.

Lenin was born in the Russian city of Simbirsk, later renamed Ulyanov in his honour. To celebrate what would have been his 149th birthday, Volga Ulyanovsk released this shirt, complete with an image of Lenin as a keeper.

Perhaps unsurprisingly, the kit proved as controversial as the subject himself. Many condemned the revolutionary idea, while others lauded it.

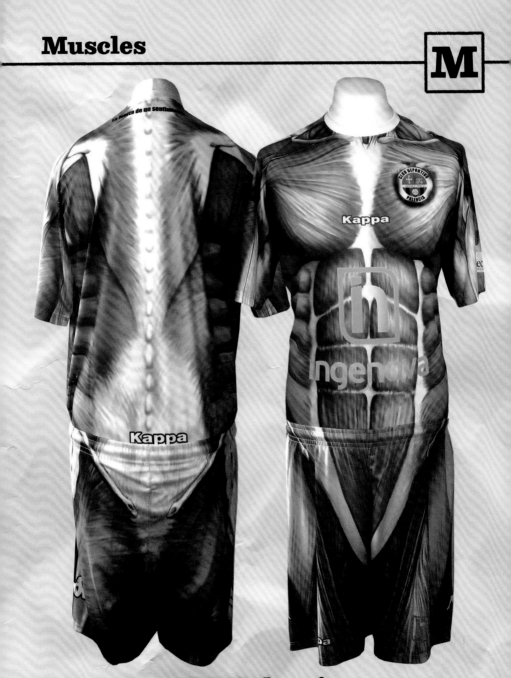

CD Palencia
2015-16 Play-Off Home & GK

Muscles

M

While some cutting-edge shirts are just garish or outrageous in nature, CD Palencia's 'flesh-free' shirt is perhaps the most gruesome ever to be conceived, the team looking like they'd been skinned alive. Indeed, the social media campaign used the hashtag #Nosdejamoslapiel, which translates as "we give our skin", the less literal meaning of course being to give one's all.

The kits were created to be worn in the Spanish third-tier play-offs - one could say the team had been 'flaying' high that year...

Initially, it seemed to work as they won promotion; though instant relegation was followed by further demotion due to unpaid debts.

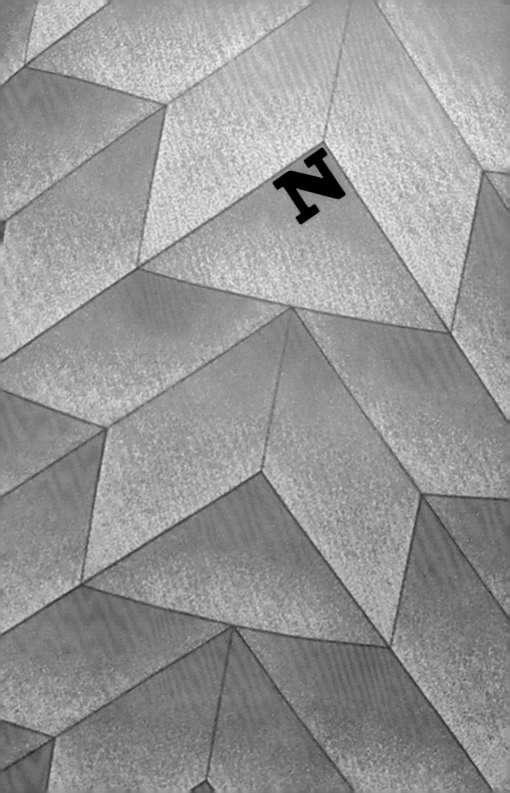

Margate FC
2019-20 'Libertines History Kit' 3rd

World-famous local band, The Libertines, began sponsoring Margate FC at the start of the 2018-19 season. When the reformed rocking reprobates decided to renew the agreement, the club released a special kit to mark the occasion.

Known as the Libertines History Kit, it gave fans the chance to have their name appear on the shirts alongside those of band members Pete Doherty, Carl Barât, John Hassall and Gary Powell.

As a proper kit nerd, having your name on a player shirt is always going to be of interest, and if that can be combined with a fantastic design, then take my money! I duly paid my cash, and there I am just disappearing round the side.

Netherlands
1988 Home

Many iconic shirts have achieved their status due to the grand occasion of their debuts – several World Cup winning shirts are regarded as classics but, in terms of design, are nothing special – however this was destined to stay in the memory regardless of the results achieved while wearing it.

While it was worn for only one tournament, it was used in every single match (and, crucially, the final) whereas the USSR, who sported the same design in red, wore theirs in only one group game, vastly reducing its long-term impact.

Add to that the orange colour and, despite being a vastly overused Adidas template, the Netherlands shirt of 1988 rightly sits amongst the best shirts ever!

Shirt Stories...

Bad Influence

I'd never claim to be a huge influence in the kit-collecting world, but I'd like to think I have in some small way helped make it a bit more... let's just say, interesting? How? Well...

Novelty shirts have been around for years and the truly bizarre all-over prints since La Hoya Lorca's infamous broccoli outfit, but the last few years have seen a vast increase in teams jumping the astonishing bandwagon in search of publicity.

When such a shirt is released, it shows up in the endless feed on kit news websites, sometimes makes headlines if the team is big or local enough, but usually disappears quickly as the next new shirt arrives.

For me, however, it kicks off a quest to attain one. Sometimes that just means setting an alarm for a website sale, but it can involve having to contact the club - not always easy when it's a tiny town in Spain whose only online presence is via Facebook.

In the case of the CD Loja 'prawn' shirt, it wasn't even the club selling them, but their sponsor, Apolo, a frozen seafood company. After several emails and an international money transfer, I had my shirt - along with the smug feeling of being the only person in the UK to own one.

A year later and I was dropping off some of my collection to Classic Football Shirts for use in their planned Fabric of Football show at the National Football Museum, in the 'Getting Noticed - The Modern Take' section. On the night, they attracted a lot of interest, especially the lovely langoustines of Loja.

Not long after, CFS not only started selling the Loja shirts, but also became club sponsors. There's since been a steady increase in the number of these novelty shirts being sold in the UK, and I can't but help feel partly responsible. Sorry... Not sorry.

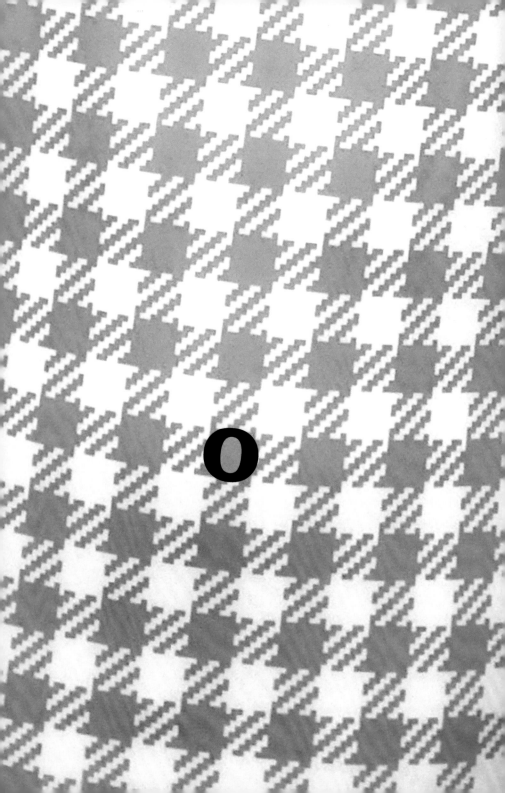

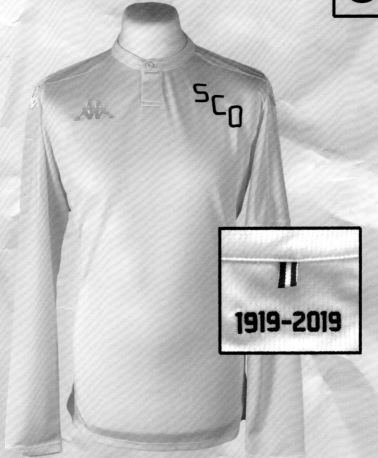

Angers SCO
2019-20 Centenary Special Edition

While the majority of shirts in this book follow the 'more is more' doctrine, clean, unadulterated simplicity also has a special place in my heart when it comes to kit design - and they don't come much purer than this.

Free of sponsor logos and with the Kappa insignia in white, the only other detail on this work of art is the club's old SCO logo, along with a small tricolour and centenary details on the back of the neck.

Based on a jersey worn in the 1950s, the match shirts thankfully retained the clean, sponsor-free look for their single use - in a pre-season friendly against Arsenal which the French side lost on penalties after a 1-1 draw.

2013

2012

2014

1860 Munich
Oktoberfest Special Edition

As we've seen with Cologne and Mainz, it's become a bit of a German tradition to release festival-based shirts, but it was 1860 Munich who started it all with their Oktoberfest series of shirts, beginning in 2012 with what is probably still the best of the collection.

The shirts have ranged from the sublime to the ridiculous, but always featuring motifs relating to the Bavaria festival - be it the blue and white of the area's flag or the traditional green 'janker' jackets.

Surely the best part of these kits, however, are the lederhosen-style shorts, which are truly amazing.

1860 Munich
2015 Oktoberfest Special Edition

Oktoberfest

O

2018

2016

2017

1860 Munich
Oktoberfest Special Edition

138

1860 Munich
2019 Oktoberfest Special Edition

P

Pants

Poopoo

SexyPöxyt
2015 Home

SexyPöxyt translates literally as 'Sexy Pants' and is the name of a Finnish club based in the southern city of Espoo.

They currently play in the Kolmonen - the fourth tier of the Finnish league structure - to which they were promoted in 1992.

When founded in 1985, they initially played in home-made brown shirts with numbers inked on, but have shifted to a much slicker all-black look over time.

Darlington
2008-09 125th Anniversary

A popular way of raising money for a club is to release a special shirt with fans' names printed within the design.

It's a nice way for the fans to feel part of the club, while knowing they're aiding its survival. There is, however, a risk with this strategy.

So it is that amongst the plethora of fans' names on Darlington's 125th anniversary shirt, the name 'Mr PooPoo' appears.

Look closely and it's there - 'plopped' right on the front...

141

Streatham Rovers
2018-19 Home

In a world where parody and reality are sometimes near impossible to separate, it's perhaps no surprise that a mock football club Twitter account constantly fools people into believing it's real. It's a fine line, being trodden to perfection by the metafictional Streatham Rovers.

The 'club', based in the 'XTermin8 Rat Poison Football League Premier Division', are sponsored by notable names such as Enya Fans 4 Communism, Bovine Spongiform Burger ('South London's Premier Early 90s Nostalgia Restaurant') and Herod Eviction Services - 'Here to help you kick 'em out'.

Genius!

Streatham Rovers
2018-19 Away

V-Varen Nagasaki
2017-18 Home & GK 'Peace' Special Editions

Peace

P

On August 9th 1945, just a few days after the first atomic bomb was dropped on the Japanese city of Hiroshima, a second was exploded above Nagasaki, killing between 40,000 and 80,000 people.

In 2015, to commemorate 70 years since that day, Hummel and V-Varen created a special 'pray for peace' jersey, worn for one match only, and have continued the tradition every year since.

This version features origami paper cranes and the peaceful praying statue in Nagasaki and was worn for their home game on August 5th against FC Gifu, which they won 2-1.

CD Loja
2017-18 Home

CD Loja

2018-19 50th Anniversary Special Edition

A Spanish lower-league team releasing a food-based shirt is hardly news these days; but back when Loja CD decided to join the competition for international shirt recognition, they set the bar at a whole new level.

Sponsored by local frozen seafood company, Apolo, what better to adorn your kit than a giant, somewhat blurry image of a tasty (yet, in close-up, strangely tasteless) cooked prawn?

To celebrate their 50th anniversary, Loja replaced their disturbing crustaceans with another local product - iced doughnuts - which, while still bizarre, were at least more aesthetically pleasing than translucent pink sea monsters.

Q

Quasi-Retro

Russia
2017 Confederations Cup Home

Quasi - "Apparently, but not really."

For the 2018 World Cup, Adidas went
on a retro trip, reinterpreting several
of their designs from the past (see
'Reinvention'); yet they'd started this
trend a whole year earlier at the
warm-up tournament, the
Confederations Cup.

Hosts Russia were given this wavy
stripe pattern design, which everyone
remembered the Soviet Union wearing
in the 80s... except they didn't.
Portugal did... and Iraq wore it in both
blue and gold guises, but the USSR?
Nope.

Germany
2017 Confederations Cup Home

As reigning world champions, Germany
were also at the Confederations Cup
and were similarly kitted out with a
retro-looking shirt.

The pattern on this one is of course
reminiscent of their 88-90 away shirt,
famously worn in the 1990 World Cup
semi-final against England.

Aside from the pattern being upside
down, Germany never had this style on
their home shirts, so this was more of
an 'inspired by' design. Adidas went
full retro the following year, reworking
the 1988-91 home shirt.

Newport County
2004-05 FAW Premier Cup Special

For their 2004-05 FAW Premier Cup campaign, South Wales side Newport County AFC teamed up with hometown rap group, Goldie Looking Chain.

Fresh from the success of their debut album, *Guns Don't Kill People, Rappers Do*, the group added their unique touch to the shirts with the 'GLC low-tec' logo as main sponsor. But the standout feature is the chain round the neck, turning the club crest into a 70s-style medallion.

Alas, County were drawn away to Caernarfon Town, who wear yellow – and they lost 1-0 – so the 'Cup Special' was never used. Instead, it was worn for two matches in Conference South, against Maidenhead United and Redbridge FC.

Recreativo Huelva
2012-13 Away

Wacky kit designs usually divide fans, with some loving the attention they garner, while many despair at the lack of tradition they entail.

Fans of Spanish side Recreativo Huelva were so outraged when this shirt was revealed that they organised a protest march to try to get the club and supplier, Hummel, to change the design, which was described as being 'something Minnie Mouse would wear'.

Hummel, in their defence, claimed they had only had ten days since taking on the contract to come up with two complete new kits. For context, kits are often designed up to a whole season before their unveiling.

Reinvention

Germany
2018-19 Home

When Adidas revealed their range of shirts for the 2018 World Cup, there was a distinct retro theme going on, with most teams' kits being a reinterpretation of something they'd last worn in the 80s or 90s.

Rather than straight-up copy old designs, they recreated them using thin lines in place of solid colour blocks, which only seemed to dilute the strength of the original look.

While reversing the direction of the ribbon fixed the issue of logo / crest placement, ditching the colours was brave and, in my opinion, unsuccessful.

Germany
2019-20 Home

A year later, for the Women's World Cup, Adidas kept the retro theme, but swapped the thin lines for a digital, pixelated style - and, personally I think it looked much better overall.

When the Germany shirt was unveiled, it was an instant hit. Many fans agreed that it was a much more successful homage (or should that be femme-age?) to the original design than the men's shirt.

It was worn in all of their World Cup matches until they were knocked out in the quarter-finals.

Olympique Lyonnais
2010-11 Away

Around the time this was created, Adidas were providing several French teams with some striking and extravagant designs, and this was arguably one of the best... or worst, depending on your opinion.

The front is adorned with what appears to be a pattern inspired by a Las Vegas casino carpet and, given all the gold trim and a poker-based sponsor, one could be forgiven for thinking the whole ensemble was conceived somewhere on the infamous Strip.

From a distance, it resembles a Rorschach ink-blot test, and if you look closely you'll see... a truly awesome design.

FC Rostov
2018-19 'Lucky Rug' Shirt

What happens when you decide you no longer have room in your apartment for that old rug you've had for years? The logical thing is obviously to take it with you to watch your local football side.

That's exactly what one fan of Russian club FC Rostov did, and it proved to be something of a good luck charm. The team had been having a bad run of results until a 4-0 victory occurred at the rug's first appearance.

Inspired by the story, the club decided to release this tribute, though despite being labelled as a fourth shirt, it remained an unofficial jersey and was sadly never worn in a match.

Rubber

R

SK Brann

2015 Home & Away

Rubber

Widely reported as being made of latex, the shirts were supposedly designed to keep out the wind and rain of the Norwegian winter. Unsurprisingly, they immediately garnered huge press attention, either in the context of the latest 'worst kits' lists or, more commonly, under the shock-horror headline 'Fetishwear for Footballers'.

What was missed in all the reporting is the kits aren't made of rubber at all.

They're a normal polyester shirt, but with a slightly rubberised coating, which improves their water-resistant qualities while ensuring enough breathability to prevent the boys from Bergen passing out due to playing in 11 portable saunas.

Scratch 'n' Sniff

Sponsors

CD Leganes
2016-17 Home

What do you do if you're a Spanish club and want to get headlines for your shirt when your compatriots have already done veg, fruit, seafood and even anatomically based jerseys?

How about reviving something from the 80s with scratch 'n' sniff? This CD Leganes kit looks fairly standard, but scratch the badge and it releases the scent of freshly cut grass.

When I bought this, did I scratch 'n' sniff? Yes. Did it smell of newly mown grass? No... It smelled of marketing lies.

Bali United
2018 Away

While most supporters regard sponsors as a necessary evil and prefer their football shirts to be kept clear of advertising, I'm a great believer in the philosophy of 'more is more' and love shirts with barely an inch of unsullied material.

Argentinian side Asociacion Deportiva Centenario went for the world record recently with over 50 sponsors, but getting hold of one proved impossible, so for now I'll settle for this Indonesian effort from Bali which at least gets into double figures.

Showbiz XI
1980s Home

For those watching football today, you could be forgiven for thinking that Soccer Aid was the first regular football gig to feature celebrities of the day - even though the Showbiz XI's matches preceded it by a good 40 years!

Kicking off in 1957, their busy programme of friendlies brought together famous TV and rock 'n' roll stars such as Ray Davies of the Kinks, David Frost, Rod Stewart and, later, the likes of Ray Winstone and Robbie Williams. From the early days, it was actor and singer, Jess Conrad OBE, who made it all happen.

Jess himself regards this as one of the greatest shirts the team ever played in, its gorgeous silver 80s sheen reflecting the dazzling line up of stars who wore it.

Ferro de General Pico
2018-19 Simpsons GK Shirts

In the Simpsons episode, 'Homer Loves Flanders', Homer befriends goodie-goodie neighbour Ned, who he normally despises - but soon begins to annoy him when he gets overly clingy. At one point, Homer appears through his hedge to ask Ned if he wants to hang out. Ned makes up an excuse and, on being rejected, Homer slides creepily back through the hedge.

Argentinian fourth-tier club Ferro de General Pico brilliantly appropriated this meme, but whereas Pirata FC fell foul of the House of Mouse's copyright lawyers for their use of Jack Sparrow, Fox's legal team have been quiet so far. No doubt emboldened by this, they smartly upped the ante with an Itchy and Scratchy version.

Xolos de Tijuana
2019-20 Star Wars Home & Away

You'd have thought that the world's most popular sport and arguably the most popular film series would have had many an encounter, but football shirts based on *Star Wars* are surprisingly few and far between.

United Soccer League team Harrisburg City Islanders have previously had a shirt based on R2D2, and Adidas released some Rebels / Empire-inspired shirts in their Originals range. These would appear to be the first released directly to tie in with the premiere of the latest film, *The Rise of Skywalker*.

The Mexican shirts are extremely hard to get hold of in the UK, and sadly the ones I managed to obtain proved to be fakes.

S

KAA Gent
2015 Champions & Golden Shoe Celebration Shirts

KAA Gent won their first ever Belgian league title in 2015 and, to celebrate, released a series of shirts based on a three-piece suit.

The blue shirt was never used in any match but was worn in the victory parade through the city, while the black and gold shirt celebrated midfielder Sven Kums landing the Golden Boot as his nation's 2015 player of the year.

The club also released a version in luminous yellow, a common Gent away colour, to commemorate getting into the Champions League. Performing above expectations, they reached the last 16, eventually losing 4-2 on aggregate to German side, Wolfsburg.

T

Tartan

Tata

Morton
1993-95 Home

The 90s is widely regarded as the decade when football shirt design lost its mind, so it's perhaps unsurprising that a Scottish club ended up with an all-over tartan print during the second 'Decade that Taste Forgot'.

Made by Matchwinner, who also created the bib shirts worn by compatriots St Mirren, the away was an almost identical version in red.

If the shirts didn't look Scottish enough, the sponsor, Buchanan's Toffee, surely adds the final touch.

Jamshedpur FC
2018-19 Away

The club was only formed in 2017, when the Indian Super League expanded and invited bids from ten cities to fill two new slots – and Bengaluru and Jamshedpur were duly selected.

They are owned by Tata Steel, hence the image of the steelworks on the front of the shirts.

The team crest reflects their owners' business, showing molten steel being poured from a smelting bucket to forge a football.

Hertha Berlin
2019 'Fall of the Berlin Wall' Special Edition

Two days after the Berlin Wall fell, Hertha Berlin played host to SG Wattenscheid and over 11,000 people from the newly opened east side of the city travelled across the divide to watch the teams draw 1-1.

Thirty years later, Hertha took to the field against RB Leipzig wearing a modern version of the shirts they wore in the 89-90 season.

Before the match, a mock Berlin Wall stretching across the halfway line was pushed over and a Trabant (a ubiquitous East German car from the time) driven through the middle. Sadly the celebrations ended there as the home team lost 4-2.

Denmark
2017 '1992' Tribute Home

The tale of Denmark's Euro 92 victory is part of football folklore. With Yugoslavia embroiled in a civil war, they were thrown out of the tournament at the last minute and Denmark, whose players were on holiday, were drafted in to replace them. Two surreal weeks later they lifted the trophy having beaten favourites Germany 2-0.

Twenty-five years later, they faced Germany in a friendly to mark the occasion and wore this tribute jersey featuring gold trim around the crest and numbers made up of the names of the 1992 squad.

A late German equaliser prevented a repeat of the original result.

Tribute

T

St Mirren
2016-17 Home

Coventry's defeat of Spurs in the 1987 FA Cup Final still ranks as one of the greatest Cup finals of all time, but it was also the day of the underdog north of the border where St Mirren took the spoils, beating Dundee United 1-0 thanks to an Ian Ferguson goal in extra time.

Thirty years on, the Paisley club paid tribute to the Cup-winning team with a shirt reminiscent of the 87 jersey.

A nice touch is the shadow stripes, which are made up of the names of the victorious players.

Chapecoense
2014 'Brazil 94' Tribute

While Brazilian club Chapecoense are sadly better known for the tragic 2016 plane crash which killed all but three of their players, three years prior the team were celebrating their promotion to the top flight, having finished as Serie B runners up to Palmeiras.

Both promoted clubs produced special kits to mark not only this occasion, but also the 20 years since the national team's World Cup win at USA 94, with Chapecoense creating a near identical homage to the shirt worn by the national side. Tying it nicely together, Chapecoense were supplied by Umbro, as Brazil were in 1994.

Cagliari
2017 '1970 Scudetto' Tribute Home & GK

When it comes to commemorative shirts, Macron have well and truly mastered the art, having produced a whole host of gorgeous jerseys, presented in large, limited-edition boxes.

In honour of the 1969-70 season, when Cagliari won the Scudetto, they released this beautiful pair of shirts, both of which are near identical to those worn by star centre-forward Luigi Riva and his team-mates.

The shirts saw action in the home match against Torino in April 2017. In line with the club's poor results that season, which saw them finish in 16th place in Serie A, they lost the game 3-2.

Cultural Leonesa
2014-15 & 2015-16 Tuxedo Special Editions

Initially released to celebrate the Spanish third-tier club's 90th year, this limited-edition tuxedo-style shirt was met with much fanfare in the media. Like many other unashamed novelty kits, it was received with large helpings of amazement and derision in the kit world... mostly the latter.

It was worn in a pre-season friendly match in support of local charities for mining families, in games against Real Sporting de Gijón and Sociedad Deportiva Ponferradina.

The following season, a second set of tuxedo shirts were released, this time in conjunction with charity Save the Dream.

Coventry City
2019-20 3rd

When it was announced that Hummel were returning to supply Coventry's kits after 30 years, there was much rejoicing among the fans.

When the home and away shirts were released, that sense of hope was justified as the shirts were the perfect modernisation of the 87-89 classic - and once a third shirt was announced, the sense of anticipation was huge.

Selling out almost instantly, it celebrated 40 years of the city's legendary 2 Tone record label. The black and white check design across the chest echoed the label's ska-inspired livery, while the back of the shirt gave a fresh airing to the 'Nutty Dancer' image first seen on Madness's early releases.

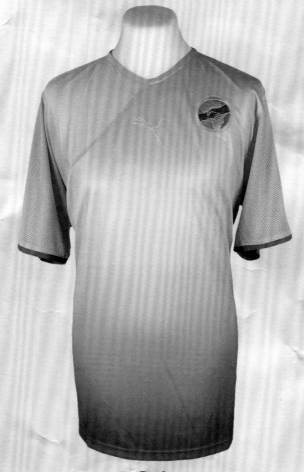

Africa
2010 'Unity' 3rd

Back in 2010, Puma supplied kits to the majority of African nations and took a collective approach to the design, using a single template but introducing details pertinent to each individual nation as a shadow print.

Extending this idea of African unity, in preparation for the first World Cup held in Africa, they also supplied each team with an identical third shirt, made to represent the whole of the continent – the brown and blue representing the African soil and sky.

As it turns out, the shirt saw hardly any action, being used in only a handful of friendlies or as a goalie shirt.

Windsor FC
2013 Home

Union Flag

Windsor FC

When Windsor FC were formed in 2011, following the collapse of Windsor & Eton FC, their first kit was a rather subdued Nike template in Varsity red.

Two years later, Thames Motor Group became their sponsors and everything immediately changed.

Capitalising on the Thames and Windsor angle, the new shirts were dominated by the Union flag - eye-catchingly rendered in red, white and green, as the car dealership specialises in Italian cars.

A Fiat 500, wrapped in the same flag design, was also available at launch.

1. 2013 Away

2. 2013 Home GK

3. 2013 Away GK

1

2

3

Pohnpei
2017-18 Home & GK

While researching a documentary on the world's worst football teams, former semi-pro footballer Paul Watson and his friend Matt Conrad toyed with the tempting idea of becoming international players.

First they identified Pohnpei State of the Federated States of Micronesia - a collection of four states scattered across the Western Pacific Ocean - as bottom of the global international rankings, and made their enquiries. The dream died with the naturalisation requirements (marrying a local, speaking the language and living there for five years). Watson applied for the manager's job instead.

He got it, too, documenting his story in the excellent book, *Up Pohnpei!*

Las Vegas Lights
2018-19 Home

'Fabulous Las Vegas', aka 'Sin City' and 'The Entertainment Capital of the World', has a reputation for bright lights, glitz, glamour and a desert supposedly full of people who've fallen foul of various criminal underworld groups. And here's a shirt to suit all the locals.

Founded in 2017, Las Vegas Lights are the third football team to represent the city, following the NASL-based Quicksilvers and the Seagulls of the ASL.

In keeping with the garish nature of Vegas the kits are a perfect homage with neon flourishes, but the best part is the Smiley face printed on the inside, just waiting for a goalscorer to pull his shirt over his head. Classy!

W

Deportivo Wanka
2003 Home

There couldn't be a book about weird and wonderful football shirts without perhaps one of the most famously named clubs of all time.

Based in the city of Huancayo in the Peruvian Andes, the club's name actually derived from the Wankas people who formerly inhabited the area.

Much to the initial bafflement of the club, replica shirts became, and remain, highly collectible around the world - especially in the UK, for obvious reasons.

What adds to the mythos is the fact that the club name is unusually emblazoned across the front of the shirt.

Camden Town FC
2019-20 'Women of Camden' Special Edition

To celebrate International Women's Day, Camden Town Brewery teamed up with a local women's side and designer Bodil Jane to produce this strip to raise money for the Fawcett Society - the UK's leading charity for gender equality and equal rights for women.

The shirt features authors Sylvia Plath and Buchi Emecheta OBE, modernist sculptor Dame Barbara Hepworth and suffragist leader Dame Millicent Garrett Fawcett GBE, after whom the charity is named.

Replicas were available with the name of one of the four women on the back, along with a number significant to an event in their lives.

England
1980-83 Home

This shirt really divides opinions. On the one hand you have fans of a certain age who regard it as one of, if not the best, England kits of all time... and on the other, there's me.

As it was Mexico 86 that drew me in to football, I have no nostalgia over the 82 World Cup in Spain and therefore this shirt.

I just remember thinking Admiral kits were cheap and nasty, and the deep V neck just looked so dated to my mid-80s eyes, but even I have to admit it's grown on me, despite it being somewhat gaudy. That said, I still much prefer the 84-87 shirt, with its understated navy collar and silky, shiny fabric.

World Cup Classics

Mexico
1986 Away

When the Mexico World Cup kicked off, on May 31 1986, I had no real interest in football. By the final whistle on June 29, I was obsessed.

As a true reflection of the mid-80s era, there was a real mix of shirts on display, some looking rather dated while others boasted snazzy modern shadow patterns and wrapover necks.

Mexico's jerseys were definitely old skool, but the oversized, misaligned crest and huge 'MEXICO' on the back – sadly absent on replicas – made them an all-time classic, for me at least.

West Germany
1986 Home

Despite the 1988-91 home jersey being regarded as one of the greatest football shirts of all time, its predecessor doesn't get the recognition it deserves.

Much less ostentatious, with a simple wrapover round neck, it was the first German shirt to feature any colour other than black and white. Here, the black, red and yellow of the German flag provided beautifully subtle trim on the neck and cuffs.

The kit was robbed of its big moment in the final against Argentina, when West Germany had to wear their green change shirts.

Brazil
1985-88 Home

While most football fans seem to love the classic Brazil look of the plain yellow shirt and green crew neck, I've always preferred this version, with its thin V neck and collar. Despite already looking slightly dated when first used in 1985, it went on to serve for another three years.

The small circular logo on the crest is an advert for Brazillian coffee (Café do Brasil), which was unsurprisingly removed, at FIFA's insistence, for the World Cup, though it still managed to sneak on to some shirts in the earlier rounds.

The shirt saw action in what many considered to be the greatest match at Mexico 86, the quarter-final against France, which Les Bleus won on penalties.

Argentina
1986 World Cup Home

It's hard to see this shirt without also picturing Diego Maradona cradling the FIFA World Cup trophy, after leading Argentina to victory in the 1986 final.

Having been 2-0 up with only six minutes to go, they found themselves facing extra time after West Germany scored twice in quick succession. However, a Jorge Burruchaga goal sealed the win only two minutes later.

Oddly, José Brown started the final in a shirt with sleeve cuffs, despite the shirt design not featuring them.

The shirt above is sadly only a modern remake as I don't yet own an original.

Argentina
1986 World Cup Alternative Away

Argentina played Uruguay in the second round at Mexico 86 and, though they won, manager Carlos Bilardo was unhappy with the effect the afternoon heat had on his players.

Facing a midday kick-off in the quarter-final against England, he sourced two generic Le Coq Sportif shirts from a local sports shop, and legend has it that Maradona chose which they would wear. A set of old AFA badges were then sewn on, NFL-style glittery numbers applied, and the rest is history.

The shirt in my collection is a modern replica, but see the 'Almost Famous' section for an example of the shirts they did use.

World Cup Classics

Argentina
1990 Home

After the glory of the 86 shirt, I had high hopes for this, and was bitterly disappointed. The neck was outdated, the central stripe was blue again and it was only years later I realised it was an airtex shirt!

Hopes were also sky high for the team, but this was soon put sharply into perspective with a 1-0 defeat to Cameroon in the opening match.

In spite of this inauspicious start, through somewhat cynical play and several penalty shootouts, they somehow ended up in the final...

Argentina
1990 Away

Four years after winning the World Cup in arguably one of the greatest ever finals, Argentina and West Germany met again, but this time the match proved to be the polar opposite.

Argentina had two men sent off and the match was only settled by a questionable late German penalty, ironic given the South Americans had been playing for penalties.

The shirt itself (this one is a modern replica) was made from the same airtex material as the home shirts, in order to combat the Italian heat.

West Germany
1988-91 Home

Despite being more famous for being worn when West Germany won the World Cup in 1990, this shirt made its tournament debut two years earlier at Euro 88, where it could so easily have been overshadowed by Adidas's other offering sported by the Netherlands and the USSR.

Prior to this, West Germany hadn't made much use of their other flag colours, red and yellow - yet, suddenly, the usually straight-laced Germans graced the pitch looking the epitome of style.

It not only lasted a lengthy four years, but also served as the first home shirt for the newly reunified Germany.

USA
1994 Home

The kits unveiled by the USA as host nation of the 1994 World Cup could not have been more All-American if they'd tried.

The change shirt consisted of a denim-look shirt, complete with white stars spread across it, and has become an all-time, and very expensive, classic. The home shirt completed the other part of the Stars and Stripes with the rippling flag effect, seen above.

Most people assumed this was the away shirt as, despite being the designated home side, the team wore the starry kit for all three of their group games. The only outing for the stripes was the 4th July second-round defeat to Brazil.

Nigeria
2018-19 Home

In the history of classic World Cup shirts, it's usually the case that they become famous due to a memorable victory (England 66, Brazil 70, etc) or something altogether more infamous (Argentina's 'Hand of God' shirt), though others simply achieve iconic status in their own right.

A perfect example is the aforementioned World Cup 94 USA kits. The team exited in the second round, but the stars-and-stripes kits are well remembered.

The same applies here. An instant classic, despite only being worn for one match as Nigeria turned out in their change shirt against Croatia and Argentina, and then failed to make it out of the group.

World XI
1987 Football League Centenary Special

To celebrate 100 years of the Football League, the FA staged a series of events, the 'highlight' of which was a Football League XI v a Rest of the World XI.

Stars such as Maradona, Platini and Lineker (playing for Barcelona at the time) lined up alongside each other for the Rest of the World side while the League XI featured the likes of Clive Allen, Peter Beardsley and Pat Nevin. Even Coventry's keeper, Steve Ogrizovic, made an appearance as a sub, replacing Peter Shilton.

Goals from Bryan Robson and Norman Whiteside saw the League XI win the match 3-0.

Íbis Sport Club
2016 Away

What does a team have to do to be officially recognised by the Guinness Book of Records as the 'Worst Team in the World'? How about going three years and 11 months without winning a game in the Brazilian League? That's what Íbis Sport Club managed to achieve between 1980 and 1984.

In late 2017, this reputation was under threat with the team suddenly finding winning form. Having won three matches in a row, they stood on the verge of a record-breaking fourth, causing some fans to protest at what they saw as losing the spirit of the club.

Perhaps thankfully, the next game ended in a dull and rather forgettable draw.

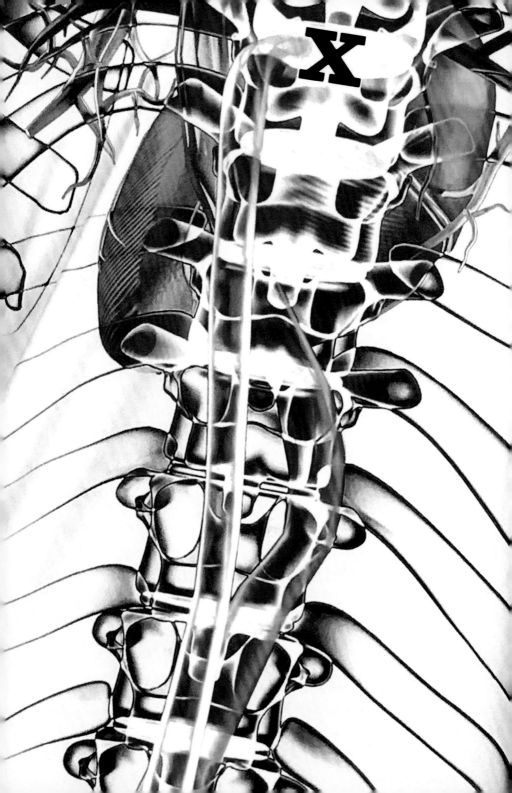

FC Santa Claus
2009 Home

FC Santa Claus is a real football club, formed in 1993. They're based in Rovaniemi, Lapland, just six kilometres from the Arctic Circle.

After only a year, they won the Midnattsolscupen (Midnight Sun Cup), a tournament between teams from northern Sweden, Finland, Norway and occasionally Russia. The matches are played during the late evening, and as the name suggests, midnight, taking advantage of the light nights in the area.

This shirt was worn in the club's first season back in the third tier of the Finnish football league structure since 2000, having won promotion the previous year.

CF Zamora
2018-19 3rd & GK

Following on from their extraordinary Astorga Hulk and Palencia muscle kits, Kappa delved further into the anatomical world with this 'human circulatory system' design for Spanish fourth-tier side, Zamora.

Meant to represent the lifeblood that flows throughout the club, the crest sits literally at the heart of the shirt. Despite being released in October, it was stressed that it was definitely nothing to do with Hallowe'en!

The wording on the reverse translates as: "The blood, that reddish fluid that transports life through our body, which is born and flows from the heart to nourish our emotions and feelings."

Noël 2012

FC Sion
2012 Christmas Special

Several German clubs, including Werder Bremen and Borussia Dortmund, have a tradition of releasing winter or Christmas shirts down the years. In 2012 the Swiss side FC Sion decided to follow suit, and released this festive kit.

Perhaps the club wanted to celebrate the start of a new era as the previous few years had seen them beset with a lengthy transfer ban, exclusion from the Europa League and a 36-point penalty.

The latter meant they ended up in the relegation play-offs that season as opposed to finishing third, which would have seen them qualify once again for the Europa League. Merry Christmas and a happy New Year!

Z

Zebras
Zips

MSV Duisburg
2009-10 Away

Duisburg - or Meidericher Spielverein 02 e. V. Duisburg, to be entirely accurate - were founding members of the Bundesliga in 1963, though since the 1980s, have bounced around the top three divisions, earning a reputation as an 'elevator club'.

Their traditional home colours are blue and white stripes, hence the Zebras nickname, though it was only in the late 90s that the club adopted the animal as part of its crest. The previous badge was made up of a stylised MSV, which more closely resembled a swan and is still used alongside the, much cooler, Zebra.

Hannover 96
2005-06 Home

Innovation in the kit world can bring mixed results. Advances in fabric technology have forever changed how football shirts are made but, on the flip side, there's that Cameroon onesie.

Zips crop up every so often on shirts, usually as an alternative to a buttoned collar, but rarely have they been used as a means of entry into the shirt.

While they were essential on the aforementioned Cameroon all-in-one, this zip, which runs the full length of the shirt, seems a bit like overkill.

FC Zulu
2004-06 Home

FC Zulu was a Danish television programme which ran for two seasons between 2004 and 2006. The idea behind it was to take 16 people, labelled nerds, who had never played football before, and train them for three months before playing a game against top pro side, Copenhagen.

Despite conceding six goals, the nerds did manage to score in the match, much to the amazement of pretty much everyone!

The Emmy-nominated show was recreated in other countries as *FC Nerds*, and season two in Denmark saw FC Zulu play the Swedish version, FC Z. The originals beat the newcomers 6-0. Knocked the spots off 'em, you might say.

Author

Richard Johnson is the co-founder of football nostalgia blog, The Football Attic. He has been obsessed with football shirts for nearly 35 years, is a regular guest on kit podcasts and has appeared on the radio to talk about football shirts numerous times.

Richard has written for the Coventry City matchday programme and *Backpass* magazine, and has contributed football shirts from his own 700-strong collection to several national exhibitions.

Acknowledgements

My lovely wife, Joanna, who was always on hand to offer support and encouragement. "Have you finished that book on nylon dishcloths yet?"

Derek Hammond and Gary Silke at Conker Editions for all their help, guidance and constant enthusiasm.

My hardcore support group, who not only kept me sane, but also gave endless advice and opinions: John Devlin (truecoloursfootballkits.com), Chris Oakley (kitbliss.co.nz) and Jé Francis Handley (designfootball.com).

My small band of helpers who for three years suffered endless questions about fonts, layouts and many other things: Phil Shelley (Old Football Shirts), Russell Osborne, Colin Forde, Mark Pritchard (CCFC Shirts), Malky (TheDonsPool) and Steve Halliwell.

For modelling all the shirts: Larry, the legendary Football Attic mannequin.

Finally, everyone else who helped, whether giving support and information or helping me find those rare shirts: Rob Stokes, Peris Hatton, Clayton Stone, Alan Gibson, Brook Miller, Shane Jackson, Joaquín Vega (CREMAyGUINDA), НАТАЛЬЯ ИГОЛКИНА, Rich Nelson, Arjan Wijngaard, Brook Miller, Shane Jackson, Jess Conrad MBE, Hernan from MuseoRacingClub, Guillermo (FC Mena), Ramon (CD Loja), Sergio (CD Pinzon) and all at Athletico Astorga, J David Ponce and all at Daen Sport, Paul Watson (Up Pohnpei) and Moussa from Hummel.

As usual, a host of excellent football websites have proved invaluable for information on the shirts featured. In no particular order: oldfootballshirts.com, classicfootballshirts.co.uk, vintagefootballshirts.com, footballshirtculture.com, historicalkits.co.uk and footyheadlines.com.

Teamwork...

umbro

Emanuele Bordoni | Joanne Exeter | Marley Mullan | Ian McGill
Jonathan Siddle | Doug Bierton | Yui Tanaka | Matthew Walsh
Simon Peach | Sandra & Bill Holmes | Nantakwang Sirasoontorn
Robert Bugter | Andy Lee | Wayne Tomlinson | Rik Keepers-Heath
Alan McClymont | Darren Eckersley | Martijn van Zijtveld
Roy Clark | Jovan Vincic | William Harper | Planet Retro Shirts
Simon Mitton | Mark Wilcox | Prairie Rose Clayton | Eivind Aarre
Paul Arnold | Sean Woodman | Scott Smillie | Paul Russell
Bedale AFC & Heck Foods | David Goodwin | Cam Melling
Richard & Henry Day | Andy Rockall | Phil Delves | Ray Evans
Regina Joseph | Thomas Quigley | Ian Hamilton | David Hartrick
Keith Swindell | Chris Allport | David Sawyer | Gianmarco Lotti
Colin Perry | Ignacio Gomez | Peris Hatton | Michael Nussey
Phillip Bell | Andrew McKie | Keith Murphy | Keith Fordyce
Andrew Culpin | Lucas Dance | Martin Berry | Andy Lawson
Christian Parlee | Maurice Ryan | Pedro Almeida | Brad Lloyd
Matthew Lumb | Daniel Hall | Jamie Marler | Michael Dowling
Neville Wylie | YourFootballProgramme.co.uk | Simon Robertson
Sam de Hoon | J David Ponce | Daen | Gary Barnes
TSPN Calcio | Anthony Hodgetts | Jeff Maysh
Kevin Parks | Jé Francis Handley | David Wallis
Mirabel Zuma Carey | Javier Chernijovsky
Ian Mailloux | Christopher Pender
Martin Hampton | Gerard Butler
Daniel Hennell | Brian Allinson
Noam Thelliez | Jeremy Jacobs
Kristin Knowles | Jeffrey P
Nesker | Frank Fiumara
Aron Complin | Mark Hinkley
Ben Ramsey | Paul Ramsey
Marcelo Silva